Cornbread Memories 2:

Home of Cotton, Catfish, and Hot Tamales!

Stories from the heart about growing up in the Mississippi Delta

By

Ron Kattawar

Acknowledgements

First and foremost, I would like to thank all of my Facebook and Greenville friends that encouraged me to put memories to paper. This second book is the result of their faith in me.

Next, Carol Cauley Kattawar, a classmate from Coach Ferguson's eight grade math class at EE Bass. We have been joined at the hip ever since. Her tolerance and patience is amazing. 47 years, WOW!

Danny Thomas, has been a good friend since we first met on the job at Northwest Airlines. Danny's hidden talent, as it turns out, is an avid English language devotee. Thanks to Danny's eagle eye and understanding of hanging participles, the book text is kept proper. Danny is one of those rare finds that I call a Giddy-Up friend. He is always ready to take on the next project, without question. Giddy-up. Truly a cherished and rare friend.

A very special thank you to our beautiful daughter, Kimberly Kattawar Mahfouz, an excellent writer and a dream daughter. Kim's organizational skills and dedication to a project are awesome to observe. Under her pen name, Kim Katt, she writes intriguing and fascinating young adult books as well as being a master at publishing logistics. Without her help, I would be lost.

And then there's Joyce Dixon. I stumbled onto Joyce when I first put pen to paper. According to Joyce, my writing showed promise but would need a great deal of practice and focus. It was she, in her eternal optimism that held my hand through the disappointments and trials that most every writer encounters. She never quit on me and as a direct result, I never quit on myself. Thank you Joyce, for being that voice that told me to hang in there and keep writing.

A group of fine people that believe in me. Any person, writer or not, would be honored to have such a team of loyal friends.

Dedication

This book is dedicated to my oldest sister, Frances Kattawar Jolly. We lost Fran to ovarian cancer seven years ago. I still ache to hear her magical voice, see her beautiful dancing eyes and bright smile. She was the most positive, upbeat person I've ever known. As a child, she watched over me. There's no doubt in my mind that she still watches over me.
Fran, this book is for you!

Table of Contents

Acknowledgements	2
Dedication	3
Copyright	4
Table of Contents	5
Introduction	7
Hook a Bumper	8
Sadie Hawkins Day	13
GARLIC SLAW	16
FRIED BOLOGNA	17
CHICKEN AND DUMPLINGS	20
Early T.V.	21
SHRIMP AND RICE	25
Delta Honky Tonks	26
MOM'S MEATBALLS	30
Disappearing Childhood	31
LENTILS AND RICE (JUDRAH)	35
Walking among the Tombstones	36
PINTO BEANS	39
Barefooting	40
MOTHER'S SALAD	43
Late Bloomers	44
SLAW-TA	47
Destiny	48
TABOULI	51
Karma 101	52
MOM'S HOMEMADE CHILI	55
Wishbone	56
STEAK AND NOODLES	60
Home Visit	61
FRIED SPINACH PIES	63
Fishing for a Date	64
MISSISSIPPI MUD CAKE	67
Super Supper	68
COCONUT PIE	71
Mr. Walker's Senorita	72
DUMP CAKE	75

Homeward Bound	76
HOPPING JOHN	81
Dear Emily	82
APRICOT CHICKEN	87
Sneaking Out	88
CHUCK ROAST	91
Toys and Trials	92
RIBS	95
Look Deeper	96
PEA PICKING CAKE	99
Tubing	100
FRENCH COCONUT PIE	105
Great Dame	106
Giddy Up!	111
Be Honest	116
Live the Golden Rule	120
Ride if You Dare	124
Traditionally Polite	128
My Mississippi	131
Coming Home	135
Unsinkable	138
BUTLAWA	143
Thank You	146

Introduction

In case you missed the introduction in "Cornbread Memories", book one, I was invited to join a Facebook page titled, "Greenville, the way we remember it."
After reading a few memories posted by people who grew up in Greenville, I posted a few memories of my own, which were well received. It became a Sunday thing. Every Sunday I would post another memory and in a very short period of time, a number of readers began asking me to compile my memories into a book. A few months later, "Cornbread Memories" went to print.

What has happened since writing the first book is the flood gates of childhood memories have opened. Soon, I began to collect memories for a second book. As we prepare this book for publication, "Cornbread Memories 3" is in the works.

I am blessed with a great memory and often go back and touch a magical time in a magical place that was populated with indelible characters. A time that helped shape mine and many other's future.

Perhaps, there is no perfect childhood hometown, or maybe all hometowns have their own magic, but Greenville for me was a bare foot walk in cool clover. The times, the places and people were as gentle as a breeze that barely stirs a leaf. The profound wisdom and loving care experienced in Greenville will reside in our hearts forever.

My mission is to take you back to those wonderful times, people and events that formed and shaped a generation of loyal, Greenville loving people that smile when their hot cornbread hits a glass of cold milk.

In the calm of the day when all is breathlessly quiet; be still and listen. The past will whisper who we are.

Ron Kattawar

"Hook a Bumper"

It was a phrase I lived with for many years. I had just turned fifteen, anxious to get my driver's license and finally convinced my dad to allow me to drive his car around the block. At the time, around the block was a big deal. If you were buying a car, the first thing you did was drive it around the block to show it off.

Mom and Dad had six kids and for years he rode a Schwinn bike to work. We couldn't afford a car. When Dad finally reached that point in his life that he could afford to own a car and retire his Schwinn, you can only imagine his pride in that 1947 Plymouth. It was well used and the only fancy thing about it was the Plymouth insignia on the trunk. Not to my dad. To him, it was a brand new Cadillac. He pampered "Nellie" like she was dipped in gold. She was a dream on wheels. For years he rode his bike in the worst of weather, from 152 North Poplar to the U.S. Gypsum Mill, where he earned a small salary to support a large family.

A few months into his first car, but still very new ownership, I had the audacity to ask him if I could practice driving for my upcoming driver's license test. The soft sell plea was, "just around the block, once, please."

After a few weeks of my borderline badgering, he relented. Guys have a built in selective memory base to draw on and there are only special memories that have earned the top five. That first driving lesson, first kiss, the first paycheck and the others we'll leave resting where they belong. I can see that day in pure clarity and can still hear my dad's genuine concern for his "Nellie." The Plymouth had a steering wheel the size of Nebraska. I recall feeling very small. The tension in the car was greater than when Mohammed Ali hit the canvas for the first time.

Before I was permitted to insert the key, Dad took his time and explained every function, rear view mirror, hands spaced just so, at the 10 and 2 o'clock position. I remember placing my hands on the huge steering wheel, preparing myself to drive for the very first time. My arms were open wide, as if we were old friends, getting ready to give each other a hug. Reality came back hearing my dad's endless drill of hand signals given with the left arm out the driver's side window. Repeat and repeat. He had to be completely satisfied that I had a firm grasp of what I was about to do.

When I mastered his over anxious repeated tasks and tests I had permission to crank the car. With my feet firmly on the brake and clutch, I pulled the large metal arm into first gear and slowly began to ease off the clutch. There was a lurch and an abrupt stop. The engine died and I could have easily done the same. I thought for sure Dad would ask for the keys. He didn't. He calmly explained the rhythm of the clutch and the gas pedal using his hands to demonstrate, raising one and lowering the other in a seesaw motion.

Now, one thing I knew I had was rhythm. What I didn't have was THAT particular type of rhythm requiring a rotation of pressure from one petal to the other. "Try it again." I could hear the dread in his voice.

I turned the key, started the car, eased off the clutch and pulled into an empty Poplar Street; left hand signal, check. Dad had an unusual head swivel, managing to look in nine directions all at the same time. Half way down the block, one car in the oncoming lane caused him to lean close to me to be sure I didn't commit a head on. He eased his hand off of the steering wheel after the oncoming car had passed by. He sat back, but still maintained a ready distance of grabbing the steering wheel, with his right cheek off the car seat and body half twisted towards me.

Driving that first block was harder on him than it was on me and I was so nervous my stomach muscles were vibrating. Out of the corner of my eye I could see him tense up as I approached the intersection of Poplar and Washington. The light was green. I gave the left arm up to signify a right turn and proceeded around the corner onto Washington Avenue. There were cars aplenty coming and going. Dad was anxious as he eased over closer to me. "Now slow down. You have to watch the car in front of you. If you see brake lights, you brake. Go slow, we are downtown and everybody drives slower here." A car whizzed by us obviously in a hurry. Evidently, he didn't get the slow driving memo. I can't record what my dad said, so, I'll leave that up to your own thoughts. Let's just say he wasn't pleased that some idiot decided we were going too slow and veered around us dodging oncoming traffic. "That's exactly the way I DON'T want you to drive."

As we neared the World War II Monument, the only traffic was a couple of cars waiting to pull out onto Washington from the Downtowner Motel. Dad willed them to sit tight until we got past them. "Slow down and make your turn gently." I couldn't have been driving more than three miles an hour. As I turned the corner I gassed it up a bit and shifted into second. "Slow down, you are driving too fast." It was the first time I actually shifted into second as I turned onto Walnut Street.

Walnut was clear of any traffic and for the first time I actually shifted to third. That was a short block as Dad and I eased up on our personal tensions. Mohammed Ali got up off the canvas. "Slow down, you are going too fast to make your turn." I eased off the gas, dropped down to second as I eased off of Walnut and onto Alexander Street. Again we were met with no traffic and I managed to get back up to third gear. As we approached William's Grocery and a stop sign, I was given the command, "Slow down, come to a complete stop, look both ways and when you think it's safe, make your turn."

No problem, a full stop, back to first gear, easing off the clutch, I made the turn safely, making sure I gave the right turn hand signal. I was pleased. Dad was relieved. As I pulled back into the same parking spot I had vacated on this "once around the block" adventure, I slowly turned to my right and felt a bump. Again, not a place to expose Dad's reaction, but imagine a very nervous man trying to teach his son how to drive while protecting his prized possession.

After the bump sound, "Nellie" stalled. I popped the clutch, and for some strange reason I once again pulled her down into first, exactly where she was before and she refused to go another foot. I'm not sure what I thought I would accomplish by taking her out of first gear and then putting her right back into first gear, but it didn't work. She wasn't budging. Dad's grumbling worsened. He realized what I had done and got out of the car, slamming "Nellie's" passenger door. "Turn it OFF!" I joined him at the back of the car. "Nellie's" rear corner of the back bumper had interlocked with Mr. William's front bumper.

Back in the day, bumpers were heavy metal chrome protectors that prevented a car to directly run into another car's body frame. That moment in time the bumpers did exactly what they were supposed to, protecting both car body frames but they were in an unemotional hug that wouldn't release one another. It wasn't a pretty sight. Two bumpers locked together with absolutely no way of either car being released from the other. Within minutes, a number of neighborhood guys had gathered around, each offering their expert advice to fix the problem. Backing up Mr. William's car proved only to tighten the bumper hug.

After a few other sure fire remedies that didn't work, one guy stood up on "Nellie's" bumper and began bouncing up and down. There was a slight give, enough so that two other guys joined in the bumper jumping and they managed to dip "Nellie's" bumper low enough that her bumper disengaged.

There was joy in everyone's heart, except my dad. He took the keys from me and finished parking her. His silence was deafening.

I figured I had earned a ten year waiting period before I was allowed to take "Nellie" around the block again. I was completely disgusted with myself.

Dad's next day at work was no different than any other, being long and hard. We were at the supper table when Dad looked at me with a bit of hesitance and said, "Let's try again." I figured wrong.

"Nellie" and I made the next adventure a less memorable one. Dad sat back in the car seat and although I sensed his anxiety, he tried desperately not to show it. He was a cool guy, like that. He placed his own concerns on the back burner and gave encouragement at the least accomplishment, like a smooth stop or a proper timed hand signal. He smiled when we made the around the block trip together. He was pleased that his youngest had met the challenge of yet one more step towards becoming a responsible young adult.

His arm around my shoulder as we entered the house never felt so good.

Love a child more than things.

Sadie Hawkins Day

Back then, girls waited for boys to invite them to a dance. That all changed when Sadie Hawkins Day rolled around. Vaguely, I recall she came from the Lil Abner comic strip and she would go after her man. She didn't wait for his invite, she extended her own. Once a year barriers were broken down and the girls had their one chance to invite the guy of her choice to the Sadie Hawkins dance. The air was filled with baited anticipation.

There was a lot going on back then. It went beyond a sock hop at E.E. Bass gym. For example, guys were taught Southern courtesies like opening a door and allowing a lady to pass though first. We stood when a lady stood or entered a room. Being polite is what we called it back then. It's not a word tossed around a lot now a days but back then being polite was the mark of good home training. Even the Boy Scouts taught the young men to acknowledge and extend all courtesies to which we thought was the weaker sex.

We obviously didn't get everything right back then, especially the weaker sex thing. But we were genteel and treated females with dignity and respect. We placed women on a pedestal.

Girls and women may have not known that the guys had a separate code of conduct when it was just the guys hanging out. We reserved the "pull my finger" stunt for when ladies were not present. I think it's a courtesy that some of us retain, unless bed sheets are involved.

Women, to me, seem to have gone on the offense. If a guy holds a door open or goes to pay for lunch, women strike back with an almost anger. Women have always been a mystery, but not accepting Southern genteel courtesies leaves a guy scratching his blindside.

True enough, most of the male gender aren't that thoughtful and it would seem to me the few nice things we try to do for women should be better accepted and appreciated. Maybe I got lost somewhere between the bra burning and women wearing a suit and tie.

Mrs. Paxton was my fifth grade teacher at Susie P. Trigg. She was a gentle, sweet lady that made learning fun. I liked her and it was obvious that she liked her class. It was my duty every chance I got to pull her large oak chair back from her desk and seat her properly like the lady that she was. I always felt good about doing that, probably because she made such a big deal about it. It was as if it was a surprise to her every time.

Mrs. Barnes, my sixth grade teacher at Susie P. Trigg was just as grateful. I think that time era called for young men to be polite, show good manners by holding doors open and seating ladies properly. I'm not sure why but that has all but disappeared from our world.

During our times, people back then took life easy. The worst thing you could get caught doing was listening to that evil devil music on a portable hand held transistor radio that you could buy at the Camp Tallaha's Boy Scout store as a do it yourself put together kit. That would be fairly tame in today's terms. Not many kids today would go to the bother of assembling their own transistor radio and would probably laugh at a ham radio.

What they would be missing is Wolfman Jack on late radio playing Little Richard or James Brown music. How many nights did I wait for lights out and dug deep under the bed covers to listen to the Howling Wolfman. His growling voice made me wonder just how close he was to actually being a real wolfman. In his rapid-fire, nonstop sandpaper cadence he always encouraged guys to be nice to girls and to be nice to your parents.

Problem is, being nice to girls today makes a guy seem confused, wimpy and unmanly. Back then, in the days of dragons and shiny swords, and teachers that were delighted to be seated by a polite young man, there wasn't confusion. I think there was a gratitude and a level of expectation.

Kids today are missing such a wonderful opportunity to speak to someone clear on the other side of the world on a ham radio. No, that's not true. You can do that with a computer. But suppose the air waves that make computers work suddenly ended. What if all the satellites went on the blink? I wonder how popular the ham radio may be then. It's a proven fact that everything we enjoy has become a bubble waiting to burst, even manners. Roger, over and out.

Guys still try to maintain some dignity and extend some courtesies to the girls. Some ladies are graceful and accept a small gesture of manners but it's a fading thing to be nice to one another.

In the end when everyone is at home, feet propped up and watching TV or playing a video game, manners are less important. Manners aren't for you when you are alone. They are meant to show respect for others. Besides if a guy is not well mannered he may be passed over come Sadie Hawkins Day. What's worse than going home from a sock hop with clean white socks?

Show off your Southern manners and give Sadie Hawkins a chance.

GARLIC SLAW

¾ head of cabbage
3 peeled garlic cloves
2 lemons
½ tsp. salt
1/3 tsp. black pepper

Coarsely chop ¾ head of cabbage. Place in serving bowl. In a smaller bowl chop up three garlic cloves, add ¼ teaspoon salt and pound to a paste. Squeeze the juice of two lemons, making sure the lemon's pulp is added with the juice. Add 1/3 cup of Wesson oil. Stir to mix and pour over chopped cabbage. Add 1/3 teaspoon pepper and 1/2 teaspoon salt and mix again.

Note: Pulp of the lemon adds great flavor. Take a handful of dry cabbage and swipe the bowl of lemon juice to get all the flavors of the garlic and lemon. Mom always tossed by hand. This is a great favorite with pinto beans and cornbread.

Fried Bologna

I must have been ten or so the first time I tried my hand at cooking. Truthfully, I'm not sure you could call it cooking, but for a kid that hadn't spent any time in the kitchen, frying bologna was a big deal.

We had a large kitchen and my mom seemed to occupy every bit of it. She had a gang of six kids and knew if we were allowed to linger, sample, taste and graze, there would be nothing left come supper time.

It was understood, the kitchen was her domain and we simply were not allowed to hang out while she spun her magic. With our never-ending appetites, she knew we would be like locust, cleaning off every morsel in sight.

But, at certain ages, we begin to find ourselves. We travel the pathway of rites of passages and begin to realize who we are. It was my turn to learn a bit of self-sufficiency. That grain of knowledge came in the shape and flavor of red rind bologna. All I needed was a spatula, a frying pan and a slice of bologna along with a little coaching from a patient mom.

The smell of bologna frying, to this day, makes my mouth water. I quickly learned to expect the bologna to peak up in the center. Then take the edge of the spatula and split the outside edge inward to flatten out the puffed up bologna. When it puffs, split the side and it's ready to be flipped. There's something about burnt bologna that doesn't appeal to me. Some like it crispy, kind of like bacon. Not me. I would rather have my bologna less cooked, less burnt. Just a hint of stovetop grill marks on it. The best part of frying bologna is the smell and the telegraphing of what's to come.

I can remember one of the best meals I've ever had was when I proudly announced to my Granny Hill that I could cook. She set me busy at the stove top frying bologna. She had a pie cabinet, always full of different pies and cakes, and in the center, the place of honor on her pie shelf was an endless supply of fresh baked golden cornbread.

It was on that day that Granny Hill expanded my cooking, allowing me to scramble two eggs. They were a little hard, maybe a bit over cooked but what was important, was that I cooked them. Her patience, calm and gentle voice took me step by step through the process.

She allowed me to cook my own meal, a meal I was to learn in later life could be eaten when the sun is coming up or going down. It didn't matter. Scrambled eggs and fried bologna became an anytime meal that I could cook. Self-sufficiency happens when we allow ourselves to share experience to those without it.

That night, that supper, my first, was a big step for me. I felt pride and accomplishment. No matter how small the victory, I stepped over from a child of dependency to a child that now possessed a measure of independence. It was an anytime meal that I cooked on my own.

Granny Hill knew my excitement and understood my accomplishment. She sat with me as I ate my fried bologna and scrambled eggs. She talked about her garden and growing her own food and how the Good Lord provided. She lived independence every day and was thankful for all she had.

One of her favorite things in life was a Frostop mug that my mom bought her from Charlie Weeks. That mug meant something to her. It was a gift and she appreciated the thought. She went to her pie cabinet, pulled off a piece of cornbread and filled the Frostop mug with ice cold buttermilk.

I watched her as she broke up the cornbread into her ice cold mug of buttermilk. Her spoon went to mixing and stirring. Looking over her shoulder at me with a gentle smile on her face, she knew I was learning.

It was a supper that I will always remember; Granny Hill eating her cornbread and buttermilk while I ate my first full meal of independence.

Sometimes the smallest moments are those that bring back the best memories. What I wouldn't give to sit at her table once more and bask in her understanding.

Life's best moments happen when we least expect it.

CHICKEN AND DUMPLINGS

4 small cans biscuits
1 chicken
½ tsp. Salt
1/3 tsp. pepper
2 small cans condensed Cream of Chicken
2 chicken bouillons

Boil whole chicken with salt. Cool chicken 30-40 minutes. De-bone. (Discard bones and chicken skin). Save the chicken broth. Melt bouillons in hot broth. Open canned biscuits and roll out flat, working in a small amount of flour to keep biscuits from sticking. Cut into small squares. Dust with loose flour. To chicken broth, add Cream of Chicken. Add enough water to chicken broth to make one gallon of liquid in pot. Bring to a boil. Remove from heat and put all dumplings in a few at a time while lightly stirring. Place on low heat and cook for 10 minutes, lightly stirring again as you add the chicken bits. Add a dash of salt and pepper. Cover and remove from heat. (For good measure Mom added extra black pepper.)

Note: A lot of stirring will turn dumplings to mush.

Early TV

Of all of the 1950's TV sitcoms, my favorite remains to be "Leave it to Beaver." If I could have, (and I often thought that I could) I would have loved to been adopted by the Cleavers. The Beeve and I would have been the same age. We could have hung out together and gotten into untold mischief. I know I would have been a better friend to Beeve than Whitey. You may remember Whitey always had to go home when Beeve got in trouble. Not me, I would have toughed it out with the Beeve.

It's true. I was dedicated, signed on for the long haul, and avid part of the TV Baby Generation. I knew when Donna Reed, Maverick and the Mickey Mouse Club came on and was always sitting in front of our black and white small screen TV. It was easier to sit close because in order to turn the channel, you had to physically go to the TV and flip the manual dial. Sometimes I'd change it early and suffer through whatever was already on just so I didn't miss a minute of Dobbie Gillis.

My mom and her sister used to have coffee every Friday afternoon after grocery shopping. On the table, was a freshly made white coconut cake still hot enough to melt a pat or two of butter. A part of their conversation always included whether TV was good for small kids. I'd eat my cake and watered down coffee and escape that conversation as quickly as I could.

There was doubt that it was not good for a kid to stay indoors and watch TV, especially on a sunny day. There was concern that the TV would corrupt our young minds and make us lazy. "That TV thing just can't be good for them."

But, when the Honeymooners came on...guess who was up front and glued to the TV? Mom and her sister. They laughed and cut up, comparing Ralph and Ed to their husbands. Jackie Gleason was funny, even to young kids, but I always acted like I hated the show. Kids weren't supposed to agree on things with their parents.

My parents weren't Ward and June Cleaver. My dad worked for a living, which is something I never really questioned about Ward until my older years. June and my mom were stay at home homemakers. One of the things that drew me to the show was of course a kid my age but Ward's wisdom always impressed me. It never occurred to me that his wisdom was born in a writer's room, writing the weekly script.

Another dad that impressed me was Father Knows Best. He always had the right answer. Now, of course I know his words came from writers and were not his own. Some years later I learned that Robert Young didn't like kids. That was a big letdown. He sure played his part well and who could imagine not liking Elinor Donahue.

Annette grew up before our eyes and we were glued to the TV when she was on screen. She was my first crush. I watched the silly parts of Disney just to get a glimpse of her.

What those sitcoms did, I believe, was partly instill principles that were significant for the time. The Beeve went to church, respected his parents and in general got along with his older brother. Good principles.

The Donna Reed Show always had good morals and principles woven within their story lines. Most all of the sitcoms expressed good American values. Therein lies the question and answer of the, is TV good for kids? Yes. I believe it added value to the way we viewed and reacted to situations and people and helped form our views on the world.

The Real McCoy's kept us laughing. Grandpa delivered the morals and kept the story lines interesting. He was already a favorite actor, even as a small child. Sugar Babe's accent had me wondering if people really talk like that.

Maverick was a slick sort of a modern day gambling cowboy that always leaned toward doing the right thing, no matter how much it would cost him in the long run. You always knew he would have to change his ways. And, at the last moment because that's what he was known for, doing the right thing.

Of all the TV watching, I'd have to say that Sunday morning cartoons, rolled up in a blanket on the couch watching Bugs Bunny or Tweety and Sylvester and of course Daffy Duck had me rolling around, doubled over, tears rolling, laughing out loud laughs. Thinking about it, they are now considered the classic cartoons, but they will never get old.

In the end, none of it was real, unless you watched Walter Cronkite or the Timex watch commercials where after great torture the watch kept ticking. Or maybe the last few moments of the Red Skelton show where the extraordinary comedian poured his true heart out to his audience.

I read an article once that said he wrote his wife a love letter every day of their life. Impressive! Gertrude and Heathcliff. Funny stuff. Maynard G. Krebbs, beatnik supreme. Bob Cummings and his fall down funny secretary. Ozzie and Harriet and their two very talented sons. Their show never felt real but was portrayed by a real family. Their strength was anchored in family love.

What I find even more relative is that the sitcoms were our first look outside our tight knit world. It was, at least for me, the first time I was introduced to what life could be like outside my orbit of the Delta. People didn't talk funny. I was accustomed to hearing what some would have considered a strong Southern accent. Until I heard Kate on, The Real McCoy's, I thought everyone, everywhere spoke the same way. The sitcoms brought freshness to my way of thinking outside the borders of Greenville. They did in a very big way broaden my concept of a very big world beyond the gumbo and cotton fields.

Maybe today's kids are okay playing video games. It's certainly the pathway of the future. Technologies already rule the world. Maybe there's value in their hand-eye skills, similar to life skills we learned watching the sitcoms and cartoons. Last generation labored over what the TV was doing to its youth. Now, we find the same dilemma only in a different form.

When the jury is out, don't rush to a verdict.

SHRIMP AND RICE

2 c. rice, cooked
2 lb. shrimp cleaned and de-veined
1 medium onion
4 tbsp. Wesson oil
2 cloves garlic, crushed
1 c. water
½ c. flour
1 tbsp. parsley
Salt/pepper to taste

Dice onion and brown onion in oil. Slowly add flour and stir until flour turns brown. Add 1 cup tap water and make gravy. In a separate pan cook water out of shrimp, about three minutes until shrimp are pink. (This is an important step), add shrimp to gravy. Add garlic, salt and pepper. Add cooked rice to gravy mixture and cook 15 minutes on low. Extra black pepper is great. Sometimes Mom would skip the flour/gravy part and simply add 2 small cans of cream of mushroom soup, with ½ can of water to make her gravy. I've tried both ways and the soup route is easier and tastes great, but the flour/gravy tastes better.

Delta Honky Tonks

Parents would cringe if they only knew what their kids were up to. My parents were disciplined, connected people who knew more than most parents. Of course, that doesn't mean they knew everything we did.

At age fourteen I looked maybe sixteen or seventeen. I still had that young hatchling straight from the egg look at times, but if I slicked up my hair and wore older guy clothes, I could pass for older.

I was still in Junior High when a whirlwind took over my life. I got this hair brained idea that if I walked into a nightclub with my older brothers, carrying a guitar as if I was part of the band, I wouldn't be ID'd at the door.

When we got to the club we had an understanding that if I were to be kicked out for being too young, I would have to sit in the car and wait until their gig was over. That was not a prospect I enjoyed thinking about.

I hung an unlit cigarette in my mouth, because at fourteen a dangling cigarette meant you had to be older, grabbed a guitar case and headed for the door of the nightclub. My tension grew as the band walked in and Al was standing at the door greeting the band. It was early, the crowd hadn't started collecting and the club was empty. Al smiled and shook hands with each band member, with me being at the tail end. Al was the eternal ambassador of good times. When it was my turn I grabbed Al's hand and squeezed it for all I was worth, my typical fourteen year old bodybuilder's grasp and Al lingered, not releasing my hand. There's no doubt, he knew I was a juvenile waiting for facial hair to appear. He leaned forward and surprised me with a whisper, "If you drink, your butt will be outside." With a nod and an assuring smile, he granted me access.

Once inside, my first impression of a nightclub, juke joint, honky tonk was, this is so cool! It had a strong smell of beer and cigarette smoke, and felt a bit stuffy. But the flashing lights and the juke box playing something Elvis, smoothed out whatever felt odd about the place. I helped my brothers set up their instruments. When they began playing, I sat alone at a nearby table. More and more people came in and the crowd was thick by ten.

As the evening cranked up and the music became more and harder driven, Johnny Be Good type, the oddest thing happened. An older lady came over to my table and asked if I would like to dance! I took a moment to get passed the idea that the lady was old enough to be my mom. Then a younger lady came over and the next thing I knew my shirt was wringing wet with sweat from dancing every dance. It was the next few hours that sealed my fate. I was addicted. No one enjoyed my brother's music more than I did. Every song fast or slow, I was on the dance floor. My brothers got a kick out of me and I definitely kept the dance floor active, which as any band member knows is important. The band feeds off of the dance floor, especially if there is a colorful character that doesn't seem to have an off button.

Our home was always filled with music. If one my brothers weren't playing the piano, a small record player was turning. It was a home that you had to slap out a good boogie on the piano or be drummed out of the family. For me it was more about enjoying their music than amusing myself with my crude boogie. They had notes in between notes and chords that rang true. My chords were more of a filler than actual music. Getting my left hand to do something opposite of my right hand was like patting the top of my head and rubbing my stomach with the other hand. I never got past the stage of having to focus on both hands and looking at the piano keys. I remember one brother that used to tie a handkerchief over his eyes and play like there's no tomorrow. He got so good at it that he never looks at his chord changes or his keyboard, ever.

All three brothers were dedicated, hardworking, relentless musicians. I was more of the recreational, occasional musician that learned eight or so songs and never progressed much further. One brother practiced six, sometimes seven hours a day. He was obsessed. He still is. And his music proves that practice makes perfect.

They played music at the Amory or Buster Brown's Community Center, but mostly they hit the night spots. The honky tonks and dives usually bred at least three fights a night with rough characters that came to fight when the rest of the crowd was there to throw back a few and get their dance steps on. Sometimes the Angry Bubba, (that's what we called the guy out for a fight) would turn on the band if the band wasn't playing the music he wanted to hear. Playing music comes with some built in dangers, Angry Bubba topping the list.

Alphonse Carollo. What a guy! Al's Supper Club...what a place! Over the next couple of years Al turned a blind eye to some of my antics. I was never carded until I turned twenty-three. A new bouncer/door guy asked for an ID and everyone around me laughed. They knew I had been clubbing since I was fourteen and not once was ever asked for an ID.

Was it a time that I regret? Not at all! I was the kid that wanted to grow up too fast. I wanted to taste life and grab for the brass ring. I became a regular at Al's Supper Club and had the time of my life.

It was the side of Greenville that grew incredible musicians and every night was different. Bands got their start in Al's

Supper Club. Al was the sort of guy that opened his doors to new talent. It's a safe statement that most any great musician that developed in Greenville at one time or another had some stage time at Al's Supper Club. And the really cool thing about it, I was there!

Life's best music started in a honky tonk.

MOM'S MEATBALLS

1 lb. ground chuck
1 c. grated parmesan cheese
1 crushed garlic clove
1 tbsp. ground parsley
¼ tsp. Salt
¼ tsp. pepper
1 whole egg
1 slice white bread

Mix all ingredients in a bowl by hand. Roll into golf ball size balls. (Or larger to your taste). Cook in frying pan until done, with ½ cup of Wesson oil.

Meatball Sauce

1 large jar of Ragu with mushrooms.
2 beef bouillons
1 clove of chopped garlic
¼ c. parmesan cheese

Add meatballs and simmer on medium heat for 20 minutes.

Disappearing Childhood

There are many things that seem to have disappeared since I was a barefoot, running wild heathen, back on Alexander and Poplar streets. I'm sure you've noticed that the mosquito truck that we used to run behind has sort of disappeared. Actually there are still trucks, but they "mist" and no longer "fog" like they did back in the day. The fog is what attracted us. We would lose ourselves, our buddies and our minds inside that fog.

When we ran in the fog, we breathed deep with our eyes wide open not being able to see our hand in front of us. Our arms flailed, mouths gaping, we screamed and we hollered. As it turns out many years later, it's discovered that TNT isn't good for us! I'm sure it wasn't that good for mosquitoes either. It was a kid's delight that our children and their children will never experience, unless they want to run behind the new trucks that mist. Just looking at the truck that shoots out a thin mist that vanishes before it has time to hit the ground doesn't seem that appealing. You have to get lost in the fog.

Another missing childhood thing begins with my mom having to feed eight people with one chicken. Hard to believe that a family that large would make one chicken a meal, but Mom was magic in her kitchen. She filled our plates with potatoes, salad, bread and whatever was in her pantry. She never bought that fancy already cut up chicken. Nope! She saved a lot of precious grocery money by buying a whole chicken and cutting it up herself.

Now, I know you are wondering what could possibly not be there today that was present back then? A chicken is a chicken. When was the last time you had a pulley? You remember two kids anchored themselves just right and pulled against each other to see who gets the short bone from the wishbone piece of the chicken? I don't have enough money to go out and have a wishbone dinner, because there's no such thing. You can't buy a pulley.

For years, I wondered where the heck the pulley piece of the chicken was. We buy the cut up chicken, just legs or just thighs. There's no package with just pulleys. No more wishbone. Heck I had a lot of wishes that came true on that wishbone. I would have never gotten my Roy Rogers, brown leather cowboy boots if I hadn't won the pulley bone, just before Christmas. Our kids and their kids will never experience the wishbone piece of a chicken.

There's not a kid from the Alexander and Poplar Street gang that didn't at one time or another find him or herself deeply involved in a chinaberry fight. They were daily. And in the summertime when the chinaberry trees were loaded down with a fresh crop, we spent hours pulling off clusters, then pulling off the china berries one by one when we were under attack. The clusters grew a bit like grapes with dozens on each cluster. A few good rubber bands and we would make slingshots. You pull back enough with a slingshot and those suckers burned when they hit. I can't remember ever being in a chinaberry fight and not going home with a mess of red welts all over my arms and legs. No kids could have had more fun than we did. But, when was the last time you saw a chinaberry tree? If they exist, they are rare. Our kids and their kids will never know the joy of playing army or chinaberry wars.

There were times, maybe when we were a bit older that if chinaberries weren't available to us at the peak of war time, we threw black walnuts at each other. If they were still green, they were harder than concrete so if you were unlucky and got hit with one, you knew it. They down right hurt. If they were a bit riper and you knocked off the outer green shell, the insides would stain your fingers for weeks.

Walnuts were always a mystery to me. When they were matured and all you had was the black shell nut, you couldn't hit them hard enough with a hammer to break them open. A hammer would bounce off. The extra effort to break one open was worth it. The nut inside is delicious. Its texture is sort of like a pecan but tastes completely different. The mystery to me was as hard as they were. How the devil did squirrels break them open? That would take some powerful jaws. I always avoided squirrels after realizing they owned steel jaws. You would probably have to hit a squirrel on the head with a walnut to get him to unclench his bite on your arm. Not to worry, there are no walnut trees any longer. They faded away like the chinaberry trees. Our kids and their kids will never know the joy of getting hit with a walnut.

Mr. William's corner grocery store had a glass window meat counter. I remember my mouth watering every time I looked in that case and saw a long square block of boiled ham. I don't care where you go or how much you pay per pound, there is no longer boiled ham that comes close to that freshly sliced ham. On a slice of bread that ham was as near Heaven as you could get. It simply doesn't exist any longer.

Along with that wonderful boiled ham, rat cheese has also vanished from this earth. Red wax covered cheese was always sitting on top of Mr. William's meat counter, that cheese was the very essence of what cheese is supposed to be. I've bought so many different cheeses in search of that astounding, mouth-watering flavor. I'm afraid our kids and their kids will never taste boiled ham and rat cheese, at least not like we did.

They say you don't miss your water 'til your well runs dry. It's sad but the past is quickly becoming a vast land of dry wells. All that we have left are memories and soon, if those memories aren't recorded, even those will dry up and blow away in the next gust of wind. The Judd's had it right when they sang, "Grandpa, tell me about the good ole days."

I've traveled the days of living the best childhood ever, to becoming one of those left to tell the stories of what life was like in a simpler time. There are a lot of us that traveled that same road when hand held transistor radios and rotary phones were high technology. A time when no one locked their door and folks left the key in their parked car and neighbors had block parties and kick the can was played until it was so dark you finally had to quit. When kids played Cowboys and Indians and no one was offended.

Everyone was either Jewish or Christian and no one forced devil worshipers as a religion on you and when "In God We Trust" meant something on our money, courthouses and Federal buildings. We had daily devotionals over the principal's intercom before classes started. We pledged our alliance to the flag every day. We ate cafeteria lunches, never knowing exactly what it was, but we usually didn't complain. We ate it anyway. Okay, we complained but we didn't bring law suits.

Kids wore hand me downs and were glad to get them. The Army and Navy store supplied us with Boy Scout stuff, canteens and cooking kits and wasn't thought of as a subversive group. The Scouts was an honored group to belong to. Eagle was reserved for only the few willing to work hard, not complain and follow the rules.

Life happened daily. It was a time that we understood why we prayed and why we sat at the same table and everyone ate the same meal, together. We looked forward to school and scouting and family gatherings. We had it all. Life was simple, raw at times, but the reality made us stronger. If I could I'd run behind a mosquito truck today, I would. Not the misting kind. Give me the one that fog is so dense and so thick you can't see a thing.

Sometimes you have to get lost in the fog.

LENTILS AND RICE (JUDRAH)

1 bag lentils
2 tbsp. Wesson Oil
2 c. rice
2 tsp. salt
1 large onion, cut up
6 c. water
Lemons

Wash lentils, drain. Sauté 1/2 cut up onion in 1 tablespoon Wesson oil. Mix water, lentils, rice, ½ onion, and salt in medium pot. Bring to a boil, cover and cook on low until rice is tender. (About 20 minutes.) Squeeze lemon over lentils as you eat, as if you are eating Mesha.

Walking Among the Tombstones

I was recently asked why I like to walk among the tombstones. The question took me off guard and I had to absorb not only what the question meant, but why someone who has read my book felt I was walking among the dead.

Maybe I'm over-thinking the question or its purpose but then I'm prone to over-think. I'm not, however, prone to over react. Usually, when I'm faced with a heavy situation, or what feels to be weighted, I am capable of stepping back, calming myself and giving the situation the critical analysis I feel it deserves. The book which is anchored in my formative years in Greenville is about people, places and circumstances that have stuck with me. For whatever reason that time, that person or that particular situation, for me at that moment, was profound, enough so, that it left an ever-lasting memory. For example; Scoutmaster Shoffner.

I can't tell you his facial features, if he was tall or average. But what I can tell you, is he was a good man who gave up his time to teach young impressionable kids the difference from right and wrong. In effect, that is exactly what the boy scouts profess, at least to my way of thinking. How you treat and respect people is either right or wrong. The way you take a piece of string and a safety pin to fish for survival, it's either done right and you eat or it's done wrong and you go hungry. So, ultimately, Scoutmaster Shoffner taught right or wrong and used the Boy Scout code of honor to present that very important message. "On my honor I will do my best." Your best, as he taught us is to do the right thing, the right way. He was smart to let us do the wrong thing or maybe went about it the wrong way so that we were allowed to weigh the better option to get the better results. If you don't bend that safety pin just right, your fish is going to flop off. There's a reason for the details and those details will reward you with the desired results.

It's a principle you learn at age twelve and will be used for the rest of your life in every situation. That analysis taught me that the right way, the right thing, the right results, lies in doing the right details. You take care of the details, and the details take care of you. The building that our troop 51 met in was behind the Baptist Church across the street from the Catholic Church. It was Spartan and to some much like a very plain club house. To us, it was our learning tree.

We met on Tuesday nights and my week remained focused on Tuesdays and the pursuit of more merit badges. I looked forward to Scoutmaster Shoffner's wisdom and direction. If that's walking among tombstones, then sign me up. I'm all-in for the full tour. What Scoutmaster Shoffner did wasn't just pass along the difference from right and wrong. He also set up the pattern of my having that ability and insight to pass it along to my kids, my friend's kids, or any kid that didn't understand that the details will define your results. It's a wisdom that every kid should be required to learn. With the popularity of the Boy Scouts at an all-time low, I'm afraid that my generation carries the now low burning torch and if we fail to pass the wisdom to the next generation, they may not survive an unplanned survival hike. They won't know which berries they can eat to stay alive. They may never learn that two sticks can actually make a fire. It's all in the details. They could grow up not knowing the difference between right and wrong.

Back to the original question of walking among tombstones, I can only guess that the reader felt my memories are from a time that is dead and gone. If that's the case, I failed as a writer. I failed as a past Boy Scout because I failed to point out the details. Did the reader feel that a lot of my memories are of places and people that are now only marked by a tombstone?

If that was his intent, then I am proud to walk among the tombstones because these are the people and places that made me who I am, then and now. That part I know I've been very careful to place the details just so, that any reader would know and maybe "see" a litany of memorable people and memorable places. This I know. People and places that you read in my memories are real. They are important and deserve the details to be presented and preserved properly.

Maybe, just maybe the memories, people and places of the past are viewed as dead to some readers. For them I am sorry that I am unable to sway them into believing that the past does whisper who we are and without that connection to memories, we become no better than a chipmunk. We lose all reason and the difference between right and wrong.

Make no mistake; the world is full of chipmunks that haven't a clue as to the difference in right and wrong. We have built a society that believes they are entitled simply because they showed up. Scoutmaster Shoffner has to be understandably disappointed. He lived by the code and expected us to. "On my honor, I will do my best."

If there were ever a need for scouting, I'd say it would be now. Kids need to know the details so they can distinguish the difference between right and wrong. There was a time, long, long ago when giants walked the earth. Greenville had more than her share. We had men and women that dedicated themselves to the youth because they understood the youth was the future. Scoutmaster Shoffner would be proud to know that one of his guys writes about right and wrong. Maybe I do walk among the tombstones but if that's where the truth lies, and if that is the only place we can find the difference between right and wrong, then I proudly linger and visit each tombstone.

"On my honor I will do my best."

PINTO BEANS

Pour loose beans on counter top a few hands full at a time. Spread flat and sort out "bad" beans and small black rocks. Eliminate. Wash beans in the pot you intend to cook them in, until water runs clear. Put water level 2 inches above the beans. Drop in baked ham pieces, or hambone. Bring to a boil and turn heat low and cook for 2 hours, covered. Water can evaporate as the beans cook, <u>so keep a check on water level.</u>

Note: <u>NEVER</u> add cold water to cooking beans, it will make the beans hard and tough. Add hot water, only. Always cook beans with lid on. When buying bag of pinto beans, make sure they are light in color. Dark colored beans are old and tough.

Barefooting

Sticks were shiny swords made of the finest steel and grapevines were cut short to smoke. Crickets chirped all night and locust sang their song of evening as you slept on the porch in the late night cool. This was the time that life offered more than you could do in a day.

One day in the life of a young kid, growing up in the Mississippi Delta, would be a life time of adventure to someone less fortunate to have been born and raised on the flattest, most fertile land on the planet.

Maybe it's a part of the infusion of people equals land, equals life at its best that had something to do with growing up barefoot. Skin to soil, soul to the heartbeat of Mother Earth that kept us centered. We were one to the land and land is everything. My grandmother used to say, "They don't make land any more. It is what it is and you belong to it."

The raw truth is being barefoot connected us to the earth of the Mississippi Delta. That being said, it may well be the reason why when one ventures away, we always have our aim to return. We don't need a compass, a GPS or a helping hand to lead us back to our beloved Delta. It's like a honey bee that knows where the hive is. There's no road map, its instinct. Our soul smells the soil.

We were connected because we spent our childhood barefoot, the soil permeating into our bodies and enveloping our very being. It's the soil of prosper, good times and bad, love and hate, laughter and sadness. It's loaded with sweat, blood and tears. It's the embodiment of the Delta.

I'm baffled by people who question the mysteries of the Mississippi Delta. Maybe what you don't live, you don't understand. They can't go back and be kids, barefoot and communing with Mother Earth, the richest soil that grows giants among the intellect, the artistic, and the profound. That vibe from the Delta soil breeds exceptional people and extraordinary talents.

There's no mystery. For those of us that ran our young years barefoot every summer and felt the solid influence of Mother Earth giving us her gifts of words and music, creating that perfect song of life, makes a Mississippian exceptional. No matter how much the offended world tells us how bad we are, we continue to prove exceptional with every breath.

The River and her tributaries, roads and interstates bring new people to our land. These people have been shielded from the finest foods, the best of music, literary genius, and a warm hospitality unknown in other reaches of the universe. Our welcoming arms, and more often than not, trusting arms embrace new people. We do what we can to make them comfortable and unusually free to be themselves. Therein lies our vulnerability. We embrace and trust, then so many times find out too late their intentions were not honorable. It is their aim to find a place locked in time that has not progressed since the end of the Civil War. They want us to show them where we lock up the slaves at night to keep them from running away.

Here's the only true mystery that anyone needs to know about the Mississippi Delta; we have no secrets. The only mystery is one that is created by vile adults that never take their shoes off. That grew up on concrete, with harsh and bitter surroundings. They are the ones looking for something that appears to be worse off than what they are accustomed to. They are the ones that condemn what they do not understand. To feel better about themselves they must belittle others.

Regrettably, they will never understand. I can tell you why they will never see our homeland as it is. Socks and shoes will always stop them. Bitter minds work best when they have their shoes on.

But, even for a small moment, if we could get them to take off their three hundred dollar shoes and forty dollar socks, roll up their pant legs, and squeeze their toes in our sandy loam, it is possible that Mother Earth will give them a glimmer of what we all grew up knowing.

That short moment won't make them a Blues legend. Nor will it make them a great cook, or a better writer. It can, however give them a small idea of what we feel...all of the time.

People spend their lives condemning, mistrusting and on what we call the side of the street less sunny. They are haters. They need a target. Because Mississippi Deltan's are so open armed and trusting, we become an easy target. We are all too well mannered to rebuttal.

The manners we learn are from two sources; our parents and Mother Earth. We learn to respect our elders and each other from our parents and we learn respect for our unique gifts from the richest soil on earth.

If you want to know us, if you want to feel the vibe of soulful music or a poem that lifts your spirits or food that is always a mouthful of party, you have to take off your shoes, peel off the socks, let your taste buds wonder and open your mind.

We are Southerners. We are in the heart of the Delta and we understand our uniqueness. We carry no malice to no one. We harbor no desire to belittle or hurt anyone. We simply want to be. It's something that we do very well. We are barefoot, skin to soil.

Take off your shoes and stay a while.

MOTHER'S SALAD

1 head of iceberg lettuce
2 medium tomatoes
6 green onions, chopped
2 lemons
1 large can black olives
1 small jar green olives
½ tsp. black pepper
¾ tsp. salt.

Break up lettuce into small pieces. Chop up 2 tomatoes. Chop green onions. Drain black olives and sprinkle on top of salad. Drain green olives and sprinkle on salad. Squeeze 2 lemon's juice directly onto salad, making sure you squeeze the pulp (the magic is in the lemon pulp) and juice from both lemons. Pepper and lastly salt. Lightly toss by hand.

Note: Mom showed me how to make salad. Adding olives was my idea, but the rest of the salad is Mother's recipe. Remember; always add salt last.

Late Bloomers

Greenville High was a busy place with her halls full, a flowing sea of kids moving from one area to another. Toots and flat notes of someone tuning their tuba float down the hallways, a drum mimicking a train's momentum. In the buzz and chatter between classes was the football team, wrapped up in their decorated football jackets. The cheerleaders were always dressed for a game. The really, really smart kids traveled in numbers. And then there were the rest of us, left to our own devices to survive another day of high school.

The school hummed with activities and opportunities. Exuberant students hang a wall size rally poster near the trophy cases, preparing for the loud throbbing pep rally, Friday afternoon. The auditorium stage filled with actors readying for the next play. The school band practice on the football field and could be heard three blocks away. Metal clinks as sparks fly from arcing in Mr. Kizer's shop class. Principal Hall is dressed to the tune of a major corporate CEO. I think Mr. Hall was my first exposure to what corporate success looks like.

Everyone seemed to have their own orbit and circle within.

I majored in getting C grades and making it to graduation. Can't say I disliked high school, just the opposite. It was a great place to be. For me, at the time, I just wanted to have it behind me. I was the kid that wanted to grow up too soon, not knowing the world can sometimes be brutal. I was in a hurry, spinning in my own orbit.

One of my favorite things to do was day dream that the last bell had sang its song and I would hop in my VW bug and head over to Buster Brown's for my daily fix of a frozen Zero bar and a bottled Coke so cold, shards of ice floated to the top.

For me, high school was what it was, nothing more, and nothing less. I invested little and withdrew even less. But I do often have thoughts of wonder. I wonder if I had reached out to others, breaking my orbit, and theirs, if they would have responded differently than I expected them to. I wonder if I had only taken the time to get to know more of my classmates, if they would have accepted me.

I would hang on the fence in the afternoons and watch the football team do their drills. There were times I felt I should have been on the gridiron, at least until the ball snapped and I heard the crunching of bodies. If you don't have the heart, you won't last long. I knew I didn't have the reach down deep grit and desire. In awe, I would watch the smartest kids' debate on our GHS stage and wonder if I could hang with them. There was no doubt that they did something I didn't do and that's prepare, study and get themselves ready. I can't say I was lazy. I wasn't. I was shy and often withdrawn. Besides, if I had participated in a lively debate most of my teachers would have needed a healthy dose of smelling salt. I certainly didn't apply myself in their classrooms. High school was a bit of a fog for me. My parents, like so many parents, programmed me into the thought that to succeed, you need an education. I did my part but gave very little beyond getting by; hardly a solid plan for success. My young mind would allow me to see getting through Tuesday so I could face Wednesday. Immaturity is always riddled with being shortsighted. The day finally came. We were lined up alphabetically, Rebecca stood next to me in the procession line, proving GHS was a great place to be. It was our last day and that day was the first time I actually spoke to her. I was painfully shy and she was bubbly and talkative. She taught me a lesson that day that has remained with me. You get back what you put in. You open a door and prove that people are inherently good. You give them a chance and they will give you a chance. I realized that day the cost of my shyness.

My mind wandered to that same football field we were about to walk for the last time to receive our diplomas and I remembered the scrimmages and wondered what life would have been like if I had applied myself, played football, been in the school band or on the debate team, and ventured out more to my classmates. Now it was all about to end. The end I had so wanted and all of the lost opportunities, possible friends, possible accomplishments, all gone. Behind me was the days of stretching myself and becoming more than a hanger-on to get through to that day of graduation.

Decades later, I have no regrets. I don't think I would go back and change anything because I know that's impossible. When the moment passes, there is no going back, and that moment passed a very long time ago. I made a lot of lifelong friends. I even made a B in a few classes and enjoyed a lot of the superb teachers, but I also left a lot of closed doors. GHS was opportunity personified and my biggest goal was to avoid Coach Wally Beach and his paddle. I rode out the clock to walk the graduation stage.

Rebecca doesn't know it, but in that procession line before the festivities started, she opened a lot of doors for me on graduation day. I grew out of my shyness and at Mississippi Delta Junior College, I excelled, making the President's list every semester. I took the time and effort to seek out the Rebecca's and the Jonathans and broadened my orbit. Behind me was not only GHS but the shy, awkward kid that lacked confidence.

Sometimes you don't smell the best aromas that life has to offer in the moment. The good news is, one can overcome and find a new beginning.

Some blooms open a little later than others. Go Hornets!

SLAW-TA

2 medium tomatoes
2 garlic cloves, crushed
1 medium white onion chopped
1/3 c. Wesson oil
1 lemon, squeezed
½ tsp. Salt
1/3 tsp. black pepper

Chop up tomatoes and onions in your salad bowl. Pound 2 garlic
cloves to paste, add to the tomatoes and onions. Pour oil over salad,
and squeeze one whole lemon over salad. (Be sure to get as much of
the lemon pulp as you can. The magic is in the lemon juice pulp.)
Add pepper and salt, last. Toss by hand to get all of the bottom
flavors to the top.

Destiny

When a guy is little, he can't throw worth a tinker's cap. But, like most everything when you are that young, there comes a defining moment and you round the bend of yet another accomplishment. The light goes on. You understand the mechanics of whatever learning curve you just mastered. For me, at seven years old, I could throw - but not accurately. The ball may go straight up or off to the left. I never knew where it was going until it actually got to wherever it landed. That all changed one day when my older brother was doing what older brothers do, throwing rocks at me to "encourage me" to go back home. I, on the other hand, was doing exactly what younger brothers do and that was following him everywhere he went. His rock throwing was always accompanied with, "Go home. You're too little."

One rock, small as it was, hit me on my upper leg. It burned when it hit and through the burn, anger caused me to pick up a stick and throw it at my brother. We grew up thinking that everything was played out with a tit-for tat...equal. Payback time. We inflicted our own justice. That payback stick went high in the air, and I well remember thinking that I hadn't ever thrown a stick that high before. It was obvious it wasn't going to hit him, but the throw itself was a pretty dang good one. At least it went in the general area of where he was running, which was at the bottom of the levee. What I didn't count on was my brother who was running from the stick, actually ran into the stick. After I thought I had killed him, sort of like David and Goliath, he got up off the ground with the oddest look on his face.

I'm thinking, now I've done it! This get even thing was now turned towards me. No kangaroo court. I was guilty. With an older brother, that's not a good place to be.

In my near future, I could unfortunately look forward to getting Indian scalp burns, where he rubs friction on my scalp with his fist, or the old Indian rope burn, where he would put both his hands around my arm, tightening and twisting them in opposite directions. They both hurt and both were meant to humiliate.

What I didn't realize at the time was the principle of "leading your prey." Without any skill or purpose, my wildly thrown stick hit its mark and changed everything. That was the day my older brother stopped throwing rocks at me. He didn't stop the yelling, "Go home!" But the rock throwing ended with a stick that left a welt on his arm and a stumble to the ground.

It was wildly thrown with unintended consequences. Sometimes, we seem to stumble on to something magic that leaves us wondering how it all happened. But happen it did and the rock throwing stopped. Best of all, there was no getting-even plan to make me suffer. No brother's palm to my forehead as I swung wildly trying to hit something, anything.

Odd, sometimes, how life comes at us and even more odd the source of solutions that magically appear. In my wildest dreams I would have never thought that I could throw a stick, even in anger, and hit a target, especially a running brother.

College was like that. I wanted to go to college, but only people with money or scholarships seem to be the only ones leaving Greenville, college bound. Since I had neither, the money or good grades, college seemed like a far off adventure that I would only dream about. But like throwing the stick, leading my prey and magically ending the reign of rock throwing, I found a way to work my way through college. It was unexpected magic. It was there in college, MDJC that I met the person I was to become.

The proverbial light went on and in that adventure of college, I far exceeded the average grades and remained on the President's List until graduation. By some magical intervention, I discovered that if you open the books and actually read the content, there was knowledge. Ammunition needed to excel on tests, better yet, I discovered that I loved history, literature, math and science. I became a learning sponge. College for me was like the wildly thrown stick that found its mark. New territories opened, new worlds discovered. New abilities that laid dormant now moved to the forward. I surprised myself and eagerly learned for the first time. Before college, high school was more of a bother than a challenge. I wanted to get on with my life and get that chapter behind me. Mississippi Delta Junior College, my source of discovery, became all consuming. When I walked the graduation stage I was a bit blue, knowing it had all come to an end. My mom used to say, "It all comes out in the wash." And she was right. A wildly thrown stick, self-imposed work program to attend college and what was to be a temporary job turned into a thirty-seven year career. Magic! All of it.

Who would have ever dreamed sitting on the banks of Lake Ferguson, barefoot dangling, holding a cane pole, watching a cork bob that one day I would no longer have a brother throwing rocks at me or that I would attend college and have an incredible thirty-seven year career or marry my eighth grade sweetheart, have three amazing kids that would give us five wonderful grand kids. Magic!

Life has its way and no matter how much we struggle to go against it, we discover that like my brother, we are destined to run into that wildly thrown stick.

Life is magic, waiting to happen!

TABOULI

½ c. cracked wheat (#2)
2 lemons
5 green onions, chopped
1 bunch parsley stems removed.
2 medium tomatoes, chopped
2 tbsp. fresh mint, chopped fine
1/3 c. Wesson oil
½ tsp. salt
1/3 tsp. pepper

Rinse cracked wheat. Soak in hot water 30 minutes. Hand squeeze wheat dry. Add all ingredients to cracked wheat and mix. Chill one hour before serving.

Note: Use number 2 cracked wheat.

Karma 101

The three of us, still single digits, had just completed the fourth grade and we were out for the summer. Explorations, long voyages and high adventure were in front of us. Long endless days filled with tromping through the neighborhood and discovering treasures that no one else had ever seen before.

Kirby lived a few blocks over and had a secret he wanted to show off. He was proud of his discovery. It meant that we would have to leave our familiar jungle and sea port for a far off place that we had to see to believe. We sat on my mom's door stoop, eating a tomato sandwich and washing it down with red Kool Aid in mason jars as Kirby began his pitch of convincing us his secret place was an amazing adventure that had a beautiful red tree that grew fruit we had never seen before. He guessed the fruit tree grew in some exotic lands.

The thing about summer is there's no shirt sleeve to serve as a napkin, so a swipe to the bare arm and we were off to see Kirby's secret tree. A guy couldn't explore the neighborhood with mayonnaise on his mouth. We passed Dr. Acre's office, a place I was way too familiar with. It was a place that smelled like rubbing alcohol and meant white doctor jackets and being given shots. Strep throat came to visit every time the weather changed. Often times, I would get it so bad Mom would put me to bed and convince me that I would get well faster if I ate all the hot soup and crackers that she brought me. She would crumble up the crackers and drop it in my soup. Then she would rub my forehead and tell me stories, knowing the strep throat would pass in a couple of days, after Dr. Acre had given me a shot. I cringed every time I got near his office. Another block or so and Kirby had us cut across some lady's yard. She sat on her porch with a small blanket across her lap.

Kirby told us her name was Mrs. Hudson and she kept that blanket in her lap to hide her gun. I remember him saying, "Southern women don't take no crap." I always wondered why he said that. He was a kid like me and I never thought of women carrying a gun. I shrugged it off as the adventure was about to unfold. "Y'all take care of my petunias" She shouted. Her shaky voice and that gun under her blanket had my left leg racing my right. I wanted out of there. As we approached her backyard, Kirby said, "We're almost there. My secret is the next house over." As we cleared the old lady's yard, we entered a true jungle of tall weeds and barking dogs. Kirby wasn't deterred and we pushed on brushing back the tall weeds until we came to an opening. Then it happened. It took my breath away as we got closer to a very unusual looking tree. It had the brightest red flowers I'd ever seen. It wasn't a large tree or an old venerable tree. It was more like a cross between a tall bush and a small tree, covered in red flowers. It took me a moment to take it all in. "Majestic." I'd never used that word before but it fell out of my mouth. The tree was no doubt very special. "You haven't seen the best part." Kirby moved underneath a branch and began looking around. He found exactly what he was looking for and reached up and pulled an odd, waxy looking thing, sort of like an apple and shaped more like an orange off of the tree. He tossed it to me, then another to the other guy and a third for himself. That's when the dog barking got louder, closer and there was more than one. We looked at each other and scattered, all running in different directions. The direction I took had a short wire fence with four or five inch holes in it. As hard as I was running and as fast as I tried to mount the fence and get over it, the fence gave way to my weight after I had tossed one leg over. The fence collapsed and I fell to the ground with my butt taking all of the fall's force. I looked at the weird fruit and remember wondering if it was worth the fall.

As I got up, I felt a board that wouldn't turn lose. It took me a moment to realize that the board and I were one. That's about the time I panicked. I dropped the forbidden fruit and starting running towards home, the board flopping against the back of my leg.

Being in a new adventure land, I was lost for a minute trying to find something familiar to get my directions right. I kept running and there it was, the place I got shots, Dr. Acre's. I knew then I was headed in the right direction and pushed on harder. My mom would know what to do. I tried not to cry.

Mom was sitting on the door stoop talking to a neighbor when she saw the fear, the tears and that blame board flapping behind me. She ran to me and I swear, turned me around, put her foot on by butt and pulled the board off of me. Rusty nail.

She hollered for Dad and the next thing I knew I was on his handle bars headed for King Daughter's Hospital. I was okay, it didn't hurt and I couldn't figure out what the emergency was.

Later, I remember I was on a roller bed in the hallway with five nurses holding me down for a shot to the butt, next to the rusty nail wound. I hate shots! That day I hated them more than ever. It burned and wouldn't stop burning.

Kirby's adventure turned into a series of memorable moments, and not all of them were good memories. But stealing a neighbor's fruit is not a good thing and neither was the rusty nail. But we were in a time that taking a few apples or picking a neighbor's tomato still hot from the sun wasn't an awful offense. Actually, it was. Stealing is stealing, no matter how small or large. Taking something that doesn't belong to you is wrong and sometimes you get reminded with a rusty nail.

Pomegranates aren't worth the pain!

MOM'S HOMEMADE CHILI

2 lbs. ground chuck
2 cans whole tomatoes
1 medium onion
2 tbsp. Wesson oil
2 cans Kidney beans
2 pkg. Chili-O mix
2 beef bouillons

Sauté onions in oil. Add meat and brown. Cook off moisture. Add Chili-O mix. Chop whole tomatoes and add to pot. Add kidney beans. Add 2 beef bouillons. Simmer on low for 20 minutes, occasionally stirring.

Wishbone

No one can fry chicken like my mom. She told me once the reason her chicken was so good is because she fried it to eat. The chains like KFC fry it to sell.

There's a lot of wisdom in that commentary of what we expect and what we get. It's all in the care, the preparation and the delivery. It wasn't enough that her fried chicken smelled up our home to high Heaven and brought on mouth-watering impatience, but when she walked in the dining room with a platter of her fried chicken, all eyes fell on that luscious feast about to happen. Connect the eyes to the brain and toss in the stomach and just the anticipation alone will have you squirming in your chair.

It's important, maybe vital to Southerners, to have gnawing the bone good food. My dad used to say Mom could take a piece of shoe leather and make a feast out of it. Southern women have developed cooking into an artistry of smells, flavor and visions. They take what they have and make it into something very special.

For some time we lived outside of the Southern Magical Realm and I have to tell you meals in other parts of the world are different. Their meal is like a chore, tacking a tear in the screen door or cutting the grass; something that needs to be done and gotten over with. A true Southerner would cringe; especially this Southerner. Give me a rack of ribs and step back.

But in our beautiful South, a meal is an event; something that is thought out, planned, anticipated and experienced.

Greenville sang its song of diversity long before diversity was spoken about. As a small child and being half Lebanese and half Scottish Irish, we were not uncommon.

There was then and remains today a large Lebanese population in the Mississippi Delta. You could speak of grape leaf rolls and most everyone knew what you were talking about. They've had the special meal at one friend's home or another. Meals, especially cultural meals, flowed and flourished in my South. I knew fried rice and not the store bought kind, but the essence of a Chinese family's home kitchen and a friend's invite to stick around for supper. I have many times enjoyed spaghetti that came from an Italian friend's kitchen where someone spent their entire day perfecting the sauce and making the pasta by hand. No take out. No fast food. No fast nothing but hard work and a love and dedication to food excellence. I can add that I've never experienced a Jewish kitchen. I had plenty of Jewish friends but Matzo balls and the lack of pork didn't exactly draw my interest, although today, I still find that I am curious about a Jewish kitchen. Even with our diverse community, filled with ethnics and differences that didn't seem to get any thought by anyone I knew, we all had a deep common thread and that was good ole Southern foods that everyone I knew served up with gusto. You could walk in a friend's home and smell a pot of greens cooking, knowing their side yard is where the greens were grown. A pot of pinto beans with a ham hock, steaming and rocking the pot's top and giving off a tummy pleasing aroma that you knew was going to be special. Black friends knew how to eat and I was usually the first at their table. Mom grew up on a farm. They grew their own food, raising chickens and hogs and that's where she learned to make do with what you have. It's on that farm, in her mother's kitchen that she learned how to take plants from the garden and spin magic in the kitchen. Her dad's major crop was peanuts. It's from her that I learned to love Country cooking, and it's from Mom that I learned my passion for boiled peanuts. Sounds silly, but I can make a meal from boiled peanuts.

You could say that Mom was a multicultural cook. She had the old fashioned Country cooking down, married my dad and learned from the best of the best to cook Lebanese foods. Her holiday table was set with an anchor of both Country and Lebanese. No one got up from her table hungry. In fact, when they did get up, it was very slow.

Southerners inherently seek out, enjoy and love anything that requires a gnawing of the bone. It's tradition, maybe an inherit trait that we share. Holding food in our fingers and gnawing a bone satisfies a Southerner better than most anything else. Chicken, ribs, pork chops or whatever fits the hand, spares the silverware and will leave a sauce imprint around the lips just can't be found anywhere. No matter how desperately you seek any of those from a fast food joint, no one can cook them better, flavor them better, fry them better than the stove top in our own kitchens or our outdoor grills. You give a guy a platter of meat, a long fork and step back. He's about to spin outdoor harmony that will make your tummy sing, "I'll be Home for Christmas."

But we live life fast and grab convenience for supper. Convenience is good, don't get me wrong, but we talk about longing for the good old days and we want to know more about our kids and what they are doing and we long for happier times when things were simple and dang it all, calmer.

We have an opportunity to seize the things we long for, but it requires what our parents and their parents did, planning, cooking at home, stove or grill, using those pretty, brand new pots and pans or that fancy long fork, and having the family sit together at a blessed indoor or outdoor table and listening to the kids talk about their challenges and accomplishments.

For me, those wonderful memories start in the home kitchen or with the perfect grill master. Lots of big and small feet parked under the same table with all techno devises stored in a far off place and a banquet of Southern love cooked up by caring hands.

A Southern meal is an event, not a chore.

STEAK AND NOODLES

1½ lb. round steak chopped to bite size
2 small cans cream of mushroom
2 chopped cloves of garlic
1 pkg. egg noodles
1 small onion, chopped
½ tsp. salt
1/3 tsp. pepper
½ can of water

Trim and cut round steak into bite sizes. Brown one small onion chopped, in 2 tablespoons oil. Add meat and cook to tender done. Add salt/pepper. In a separate pot cook noodles and add to meat. Pour in 2 cans of cream of mushroom & 1/2 can water, using cream of mushroom can. Cover and simmer for ten minutes.

Home Visit

Going to Greenville, May 2, 3, 4 of 2014 rekindled a ton of memories. My daughter, Kim and I rode around, making the Strazi run, riding the levee, and back into the neighborhood I grew up in. We also rode through Kim's old stomping grounds. It was good for both of us.

Later Ron Powell and I rode the streets both reliving a magical time in our lives. That, of course, pulled up even more memories. Before taking on the monumental task of journaling the days of sherbet pushups and Jack's cookies, I honestly hadn't realized how significant those memories would be, not so much for me as for others that traveled the same paths that I walked. It's an awesome journey that includes you and your memories and how well you did at the Y in their minnow program or how awe struck you may have been when Lash Larue was live on the Paramount stage, the perfume smell of the Marion Parlor, next to the Paramount, or one of their thickest milk shakes ever. Or, maybe sliding down the levee on cardboard boxes or flying the airplane at Strange Park. All in a time that didn't seem so important until adulthood. I realize now, we lived in a special time, a special place and were surrounded by some really special people. It's a time that is slowly slipping away, when families sat together at the table and ate a home cooked meal, always after a blessing and giving of thanks. "Supper talk" was usually the adults slowly but surely programming us into becoming responsible, law abiding citizens. Their conversations were not small talk but deeply rooted in moral and ethical lessons that generally ended with, "Or you'll have the devil to pay for your bad actions rooted in bad intentions."

They earned the title, Greatest Generation for a reason and if we were smart, if we were what they wanted us to be, we paid attention to their hard earned advice.

It's that elusive time in our lives that we were spirited and carefree to explore all that was Greenville. To grasp life beyond Greenville simply wasn't on the menu except what we would see pictures in National Geographic, miles and lifetimes away. Our world expanded some with the encyclopedia or in a flight of fancy with Superman comic books. But at the end of a humid, hot summer day, our lives were enveloped in our small community with no thoughts given that one day we would be taller, older and able to break the ties that bind. If we wanted to, we could travel on far away explorations, being a part of what we had seen on TV, like Central Park in New York City or the royal palms blowing in the tropical breeze in Hawaii.

The last thing that we would have ever imagined in those tranquil, magical times was that someday it may all end.

That someday is nearby. As I drive around Greenville, my mind flashes back to those days of trying to wear adjustable skates without shoes or trying to adjust the skates without a skate key. I see a little black headed kid, wild as a heathen, laughing, running and playing without a care in the world.

It's a world that can be saved in "Cornbread Memories." Between the pages, the childhood, the time, our lives are preserved forever. It's in our book. We will always be ten years old, Huck Finns of Greenville, showing off smiles that proves there really is a tooth fairy.

Horizons, then and now. We can have both.

FRIED SPINACH PIES

DOUGH

2 c. self-rising flour
½ c. shortening
¾ c. milk

Place the flour in a small mixing bowl. Cut in shortening with fork. Stir in milk. Mix dough until no longer sticky. Pinch off dough and make a ball the size of a small egg. Sprinkle with flour and roll thin and flat to a 5 inch circle. Place 2 tablespoons of spinach at one end and fold over. Seal with fork along edges. Prick pie 3 or 4 times to vent. Place in hot grease and brown both sides until golden brown.

SPINACH STUFFING

2 (8 oz.) boxes frozen spinach
3 tbsp. olive oil
4 green onions, chopped fine
1/2 tsp. salt
½ c. anise, de-stemmed and chopped fine
½ c. water
1/3 tsp. pepper

Cook spinach in ½ cup of water until water has evaporated. Add oil, salt, pepper, onion and anise. Cook 20 minutes on medium heat.

Allow cooked spinach to cool, making sure the spinach is dry before stuffing. Drain on paper towel.

Fishing for a Date

It's a part of a young guy's growing up to be on a river bank or in a Jon boat wetting a hook and talking to the fishes. "Here fishy, fishy."

That's in the early years when a strike from a bream will challenge little arms and a pounding heart. Bream can kick up quite the fuss, especially if the little guy has a cane pole and a red and white bobbing cork.

There's an art to when the bobber goes down and when to hook the fish. It's only a second and it has to be the right second that you learn to snatch up the pole to set the hook, otherwise that bream won't be going home with you.

We were kids, older kids, in our late teens when we went to the bar pits in hopes of a fine mess of bream. With a cane pole, you can feel every bit of their fight making it a large part of the thrill. You eventually develop the skill of setting the hook at just the right moment. The cane pole, setting the hook and adding in that special flavor of bream, will keep you coming back for more. Some call it redneck fly fishing. I call it fun.

If you've been to the bar pits at Lake Lee, you know there's a gravel road that runs between two bodies of water. We'll call it the north bar pit and the south bar pit, if you were standing on the road that divides the two.

My fishing partner that day was inexperienced, hadn't learned how to set the hook and had way too much adrenalin pumping to learn anything. It's strange how adrenalin impairs your hearing.

Being of the fairer sex, I had to bait her hook for her. Handling a wiggling worm wasn't in her DNA.

When the bream are feeding and the sun isn't bearing down on you too hard, bream fishing can be almost as exciting as deep sea fishing. Well to an inexperienced fisher, anyway.

Hook baited and cork now settled to a calm water surface, the cork begins to bob-bob-bob, what do you suppose happens? The novice fisher-lady in the gravel road, snatches up that poor little bream and raises her pole at full mast, flipping the bream over to the south water side. I swear I think I heard that bream laugh as he swam away. Brer Rabbit, laugh. My little fisher-lady was confused. It took her a moment to realize she had snagged a north side bream and relocated him to the south side. Her hook was bare. No fish, no bait, no nothing. The last thing I should have expected was a smile.

Now guys, take note. If you are on a "fishing date" you don't ever under any circumstances laugh at your date. It's okay to laugh with her, but never...ever at her. I say this from firsthand experience. I did the wrong kind of laughing at the worse possible moment. She was ready to go home. I had to stop rolling on the ground, wipe away the laughter tears and take her home. She sulked all the way.

Not to be outdone and optimist eternal, I invited her on the next fishing expedition, this time with a Jon boat and trolling motor. At least this time she couldn't relocate the fish. Plus, I had the new advantage of knowing I could only laugh at something weird or stupid I did, not her.

All is well. Excitement is strong in the early morning calm waters. All settled in the boat, all of the warnings, cautions and safety tips expressed, like no standing up in the boat stuff, basics, and we're off.

In the first three minutes she spots a moccasin laid up in some branches near the bank. Yes, she freaks and the first thing she did was what? Stand up.

I'm feverishly trying to back the boat out away from the bank and had to clear us under a brush line. I thought when she saw the snake she freaked, but when some of the lower limbs brushed against her, I thought she was going to walk on water to get back to the bank.

More advice for you guys that decide you want to take your lady friend on a fishing date. Don't. Marry her first and that way you can negotiate with her lawyer and maybe end up with at least half of your boat.

Now if she has grown up fishing, understands and enjoys the outdoors, and can bait her own hook that's a different kettle of fish. I would highly recommend it. But, unless you are tireless in patience and she is a devout adventurer, keep your dates on dry land.

And never begin a conversation with, "You remember the time you snatched that bream out of one side of the bar pits and..."

You could go to bed without supper.

MISSISSIPPI MUD CAKE

1 c. margarine
½ c. cocoa
2 c. sugar
4 eggs, slightly beaten
1½ c. chopped pecans
½ c. flour
1 tsp. vanilla
1/8 tsp. salt
1/4 bag of small marshmallows

Melt margarine and cocoa together. Remove from heat. Stir in sugar and mix well. Add beaten eggs, flour, salt, pecans and vanilla. Mix well. Pour into 13x9 baking pan. Cook 25 minutes or, until cake is done. Place small marshmallows on top of hot cake.

FROSTING

1 lb. confectioners' sugar
½ c. whole milk
½ c. cocoa
½ stick margarine

Combine all ingredients and mix until smooth and creamy. Pour over marshmallows on cake. After frosting, place whole pecans on top. If your mouth isn't watering, something is wrong with you.

Super Supper

I'm a foodie, a purest. I often spend some frustrating moments in the kitchen, seeking that perfect blend of expectation to match taste buds.

When I was in my early teens, I would spend my day at school, then the ball field and I would go home starving. The moment I walked in our front door, I knew whatever we were having for supper would be amazing. It always was; every meal, without fail. Mom was a foodie, a purest.

Hard to imagine in today's world but she would start early in the day and cook for hours perfecting her meal. She never settled for less. I can remember she would sprinkle down our clothes and put them in the refrigerator until she had supper cooking. Then she would pull out the dampened clothes and iron for hours. I loved the crease she put in my jeans.

Mom didn't eat out. Her time was focused on her kids, her husband and the kitchen. I wouldn't try to put those in her priority sequence, but to her they were all interrelated. When she did eat something that wasn't from her kitchen it would be a ham sandwich, ruffled potato chips and a "short" bottled Coca Cola from Jim's Cafe. As a kid I can't remember her ever actually eating a cooked meal outside her home.

I've said this before and it is worth repeating. Mom never took short cuts in her cooking. She was convinced and often said, "you can taste the short cuts."

James Middleton came home with me one time and the moment we walked in the door he said, "Oh my God, what is that cooking?"

I didn't realize it at the time but our home had an aura and aroma that automatically captivates anyone who enters the front door. My cousin told me once that walking in our home made her hungry. If you are curious what that alluring and captivating aroma was, I can tell you. Put a spoon full of Wesson oil into a pot on medium heat. Then chop up a raw onion and drop it into the hot oil. Boom! Now if you want to really drive someone nuts, add a couple of chopped garlic cloves. That will send you over the moon. Therein lays the secret of a kitchen that draws everyone in.

Most of the Lebanese dishes start off with a little oil, chopped onion and chopped garlic. The Cajuns call it "Rue." I call it magic! Once James pointed it out, I became aware. I noticed that his home, as well as Kirby and Eddie's homes, were all missing that...aroma. None of them drew you in and made you want to park your feet under their supper table. Thanks to James, I realized just how special our home was. He freaked when I told him we were having grape leaf rolls. "You mean you eat leaves?" Well, people line up to have grape leave rolls. If they are made right, there's little else on earth that can compare. Problem is not many can make them correctly. Purest. Which takes us back to being a foodie. No one and I do mean no one can make grape leave rolls like my mom, the purest. It's an all-day process. Yet, so many take shorts cuts. Remember you can always taste the short cuts. I learned step by step from Mom. No short cuts.

When my siblings want to return to that taste, that distinct flavor, they ask me to roll a pot of mesha (grape leaves). As a kid growing up, I had no idea how incredibly delicious Mom's cooking was. Maybe I took it for granted then. I think, maybe we all do, at some point.

But when we moved to Bermuda, Mom wasn't there to work her magic in my kitchen. So, when I went back to Greenville for a visit, I spent a lot of time with this foodie, the purest.

I learned the only way of doing things. I learned her ingredients like Wesson vegetable oil. You can't use anything else and expect it to taste the same.

Siblings bought small electric choppers and chopped their onions. Mom always hand grated her onions for the grape leaf stuffing. You can taste the short cuts. Hand grated onions are far superior to electric buzzed onions. You lose the onion juice in an electric chopper. Don't expect the same taste if you change the steps or change the ingredients.

James, Eddie and Kirby lingered, always hoping Mom would invite them for supper. They all had mom's that cooked but not like my mom. We seldom had a meal that one of our friends wasn't digging in elbow to elbow.

We had neighbors knocking on the front door to ask what Mom was cooking. Folks walked in our home and sat at our table waiting for the food to come out. Of course, they thought they were at Mrs. Strickland's, who ran a boarding house across the street from our home. I remember how disappointed they were that they were in the wrong house. That aura, that lingering, alluring aroma was tough to leave behind.

As a treat, a real tummy stretcher, I've included Mom's very special, over the top recipe for mesha (grape leaves is in book one, listed as Cabbage Rolls). Just remember if you change the recipe or alter the way it's detailed, don't expect greatness. It won't happen.

But if you are a true foodie, a purest and follow each step exactly, expect your neighbors to be knocking on your door.

Greatness and purest are one in the same.

COCONUT PIE

5 tbsp. flour
1 tsp. vanilla
2 c. milk
2 eggs, separated
1 pkg. coconut
1 pie shell
5 tbsp. sugar
Dash of salt

Put flour in saucepan and add sugar, salt and milk. Cook on low heat until mixture begins to thicken. Take a little of the flour mixture and put in a bowl with egg yolks, stir well. Pour into saucepan. Continue cooking until mixture is thick. Just before taking from heat, add coconut and vanilla.

In a separate bowl, beat egg whites with 2 tablespoons of sugar. Then add 2 more tablespoons of sugar and beat. Add ½ teaspoon of vanilla. When thick and fluffy, put Meringue on top of pie and bake until lightly brown. (3-5 minutes).

Note: Mom always sprinkled a little coconut on top of meringue before baking.

Mr. Walker's Senorita

Back in the day of king of the mountain, chinaberry wars and double dog dares, our neighborhood centered on William's Grocery. If you sat on his wooden steps and counted the number of times the screen door squeaked open, you would see everyone in the neighborhood before you counted to fifty squeaks. William's corner grocery store was the beehive of our world.

Some days, when the sun was so hot and the humidity was so heavy, we walked on the grass to avoid the hot pavement. Even tough bare feet couldn't stand up to the fry-an-egg hot pavement that sizzled in a short spring shower.

Three or four of us guys would gather at Mr. William's store front, sweat out the early morning heat and talk about what we would be doing if it weren't so blamed hot. We could dig worms and go fishing or dream about having enough money to go to the Paramount to watch a real live shoot 'em up cowboy picture show, in air conditioning.

Some days, usually on Fridays, everyone had a few pennies, a nickel or even a dime and we would pool our money to buy a couple of frosty cold Pepsi's and pass them around. We had a six second rule that meant if you held the drink straight up and guzzled for more than six seconds, you didn't get another shot at the quickly emptying bottle. One boy we fondly called "no neck" could empty a Pepsi in four seconds. We always made him go last. Strangest thing, his head sitting right on top of his shoulders like that. But "no neck" had a curve ball that no one could hit. He was always a first draft when it came time to dividing up into baseball teams.

He was one of the few that were chosen for his baseball skills. The rest of the draft were buddies sticking together. Most of us were still in the developing skill stage. (That means we couldn't play ball very well.)

One especially hot Friday we all gathered at Mr. William's grocery store. Pooling our money, we had enough for one Pepsi. I don't recall how the conversation turned to Mr. Walker, Mr. William's brother-in-law that helped out in the store, but "no neck" swore he had it on good information that Mr. Walker had himself a Friday Senorita. He never left the store, except on Fridays. That day he disappeared for the day and no one knew where he went. Mysteries in a small neighborhood grew to epic proportions.

Idle minds probably created the Senorita idea. No one ever had the guts to ask him...until that now infamous Friday when "no neck" stuck out the neck he didn't have on a double dog dare. He earned a whole Pepsi, if he took the dare.

Mr. Walker came out of the store when "No neck" stepped forward and blurted out, "Mr. Walker, you going to see your Senorita?" We all prepared to run.

I can still hear that bizarre, off the chart laugh that Mr. Walker let loose. He hardly ever smiled and we put our heads together to recall if any of us had ever heard him laugh before. He wasn't the laughing, smiling kind. But that day, that moment for a few seconds it appeared, Mr. Walker may keel over from a deep down, belly laugh that could cool the Devil hot pavement.

He didn't answer "No neck." But his laughter followed him to his car. I could hear him laughing as he turned the corner and faded out of sight.

"No neck's" double dog dare earned him that whole Pepsi. Four seconds flat and the bottle was empty.

Our gathering was broken up when one of those out of nowhere short spurts of rain caused steam to lift from the sidewalk and road. We huddled on Mr. William's store front steps, barely out of the rain. After the brief shower, the humidity worsened making the air thick and heavy, pressing down on us.

It wasn't until the next Friday that Mr. William's would bring out the Jack's Cookies clear container he kept on his counter next to the cash register. We all knew at the end of each month the Jack's man would come by the store and fill up the container with fresh, new cookies. It was our "duty" to make sure all of the broken cookies were removed to make room for the delivery. Mr. Williams always had one Pepsi and a cookie bin one third full. He didn't say anything. He didn't have to. We dove in like there may never be another cookie in our life time.

That Friday he lingered, which was very unusual. Mr. Walker came out of the store, gave a small wave and hurried off to his car.

Mr. Williams watched him drive off and turned to us with a smile. "The crappie are biting." He left us with that little jewel of information, as he laughed out loud and entered his store.

Turns out, Mr. Walker's Senorita was a small round wash tub with a tractor's inner tube around it, making him a poor man's fishing boat. Mr. Walker's Senorita wasn't a woman after all, but an every Friday fishing trip at the Bar Pitts.

Sex, lies and Senoritas in the 1960's.

DUMP CAKE

1 pkg. yellow cake mix
1 (20 oz.) crushed pineapple
1 can cherry pie filling
1 c. chopped pecans
1 stick of margarine, sliced thin.

Dump un-drained pineapple in a 13x9-inch baking dish. Add cherry pie filling and spread evenly. Dump dry cake mix and spread evenly. Sprinkle pecans over cake mix. Place margarine pats over top. Bake 50 minutes at 350°.

Homeward Bound

No matter where you travel, nor how long you stay, a calling back to the Mississippi Delta is a given. I wonder why. It's a decades old question that no one to this point has reasonably answered.

Sure, people have their theories, and that pretty much sums up where I am on the issue. I have a theory, nothing more. It's not something that you can pick up and measure, inspect and dissect. For me it's a question of the soul. I'll get to that later.

Why does one man put his heart and body into a farm or his own mechanic shop? Who says it's his mission in life to stay poor or better yet, to be rich? Stunning questions that escape our grasp of who is and who isn't and who should and who shouldn't. Why are some women driven to be the best they can be in the kitchen, cooking up a Southern storm, while others are completely satisfied with take out? Where does the desire, the need come from? How can some pray for hours in earnest while others go to church on high holidays like Easter and Christmas? Is there a reasonable balance that brings one to God without spending his life time in total devotion?

Now, I've been around enough Southern Baptist who profess total dedication to God is mandated. Yet, follow that dude late on Saturday night and you'll get a totally different picture of his professing by his actions. An older gent, in his late seventies approached me about writing his life story. As a writer, one can get the feel of a person usually in the first conversation, as to whether that person is sincere or prodding and poking at the idea of having their life exposed in a book. This particular gentleman wanted what's known as a "ghost writer." That is to say, he sought a writer to write his story for an agreed amount of money and place his name on the work as if he had written it.

I'm not opposed to the idea, especially considering the monetary compensation is premium. The reason, of course, is the writer gets no credit, nor does he get any compensation from the sale of the book. He could and its happened many times before, write a bestseller that pays high dividends, which the ghost writer has relinquished in the agreement. So a premium front end payment is standard.

For the sake of the story, we will call this guy Tom. Now, Tom was completely committed to having his story told, especially one compelling chapter, in which he died. A writer can't tell a story without the background. It's the very backbone of his craft. What may seem trivial to most, could in fact be instrumentally pivotal.

There's a drill down process that must be explored. It may not be critical to the story what brand of toothpaste he uses, but the fact that he brushes could play an important role. In Tom's story it does. He may have not died, had an oral infection not set in. But one can't start an engaging story with an oral infection. You have to go back in time and find out what this person has done, is doing and plans to do later on, even if he is in his late seventies. One must ask, why do you want your life story written? What is the purpose? What do you expect to accomplish? Tom's mission will stun you. It certainly had me reeling. I needed a moment to absorb his words.

His mission, his purpose and his driving force to have his story told was to debunk religion. Yep! He wanted his life story to clearly state, there is no God and that religion was a hoax. "People are being fooled and I want them to know it!" This gentle man, with a soft voice, dimmed eyes from age with an occasional shake in his farm weathered hands, wanted to take on a two thousand year old belief system and destroy it. He felt his story would prove there is no God and all the hype and hymn singing was useless.

I had to excuse myself from the conversation and catch my breath and find my clay feet underneath me. Why would such a worn guy that obviously worked hard all his life feel the need to deny God? Alone and grasping for answers, the most critical questions came rapid fire. Personally, deep down, can I write something that is so oppose to my very being and fiber? Could I or should I lend my writing abilities to such a story? Is my constitution so strong that as a writer I can separate myself from the story being told?

And the final question I had to ask myself was, am I a professional or a hack writer that takes on what suits me? An actor playing a murderer, he doesn't really kill someone, but as a pro he takes the gig. It's not like my name will be on the book. He wants to hire a ghost writer. I went back into the conversation armed with the statement that separates the boys from the men, my price for the undertaking. It was high. I didn't back up and gave him a nice round figure. He shivered.

There, I knew it! He isn't serious. He just wanted to vent. Then he came back with a counter offer. My next move was to ask more about his story. Maybe I can end the story with his questioning religion. Maybe I can inject my beliefs into his story. I was mentally scrambling to rationalize his intent and my personal convictions. He began a bit of his story. He had an infection that ended him up in the hospital. He was unconscious. They were unable to identify why his body was racked with infection and its source.

In their testing stages and frantically trying to determine treatment, he died. The nurse found him on his side and all of his blood had drained to one side of his body. There's no heartbeat. He's dead and had been dead for some time. It was much later they surmised what may have happened; the reason for his death and the miracle of how they revived him.

No one knew, nor do they claim to know today, how long he was dead. But, all is in agreement that he was dead for a very long time before they revived him. Their first concern was brain damage, then internal damage, all of which did not manifest. He was his usual self, with all faculties in place. That's where his anger, his resentment and vile destiny began. When he died there was no light. God didn't speak to him. No one met him at the gate. There was only void; an unexpected nothingness.

He was a religious man, from childhood, a devout Southern Baptist from the Mississippi Delta. He and his family were at church every time the door was open. He sang hymns and worshiped from a bare foot sharecropper's son to a family man in his late seventies. He studied the Bible and could quote chapter and verse. And yet at his final hour he felt abandoned. He was angry and he wanted to tell the world how they are wasting their time believing in something that doesn't exist.

After hearing his story summary, I knew this was not a project I wanted. I knew that no matter how I interjected the miracle that he was revived and that alone was an act of God, I knew I couldn't get through or settle his anger. That's an internal struggle that only Tom can fight.

No amount of money could justify my taking the gig. I had to back away. Had I been an atheist, I could have done his mission as he wanted. My guess is, some atheist will gladly take up his banner of disbelief. It just won't be me. The Mississippi Delta is full of colorful characters, Tom certainly heading the parade. The truth is always hidden deep within our soul and Tom hasn't found his answers. This brings us back to my theory of why people return to the land of gumbo and cotton.

The hard questions we have that send us far and wide exploring, searching, aren't in a book some angry guy has written. It's not on some tropical island with umbrella drinks. The answers we seek take us back home and to a time when we were bathed in the warmth of unconditional love. It's where we felt safe. When we stumble and fall, there's always someone there to help us get back up.

Its home. Home is where we find all the answers we need.

HOPPING JOHN

1 8oz pkg. dried black-eyed peas
1 ½ pound hambone
1 small white onion
1 tsp. salt
½ tsp. pepper
1 c. instant rice
1 large can whole tomatoes

Place peas in large saucepan and cover with boiling water. Add hambone, onion, salt and pepper. Simmer for 1 hour and 15 minutes. Place rice over pots contents, adding enough water to cover rice. Bring to a boil. Cover and remove from heat. Allow to stand until rice is tender and flaky. Stir in tomatoes. (This last step is cooking the instant rice in the pots mixture.)

Let sit for five minutes for all flavors to meld together and serve hot.

Dear Emily

Not so long ago a couple came to me and asked that I write a screenplay about their friends, both now deceased. Thing is, this couple had a magical experience, a once in a lifetime love story that transcended death. They told me the magic moment about their friends in less than three minutes. It was very moving. Moving or not, magical or not, I had to write a ninety minute movie based on a three minute description of an event that could only happen to two very special people, sharing a love so deep, so emotional that death itself could not separate them. As any good writer knows, you can't write something that you aren't familiar with. I knew what I had before me was a long journey of discovering who this couple was. That meant watching their home movies, viewing hundreds of snapshots, talking with their friends and family and more or less finding the shoes that they wore and walking their familiar ground. While sitting on his Harley in his driveway, I envisioned him doing the same, looking at his home and backyard. How a guy manicures his yard speaks a lot about his personality. I paid attention to details or the lack of, how the Harley handled, and who sold him the Harleys that he owned, which as it turned out were many. The Harley distributor had become a close friend and revealed a lot of the guy's nature. She was a school teacher, the last person I would imagine on the back of a Harley making cross country trips. She was small and quiet, but on the Harley weekends she became a real spitfire, decked out in full body leather. There are a lot of underground worlds and Harley is no exception. The notion that folks that ride Harleys are unclean, unshaven bullies may have been true decades ago but in today's world, they are yuppie-like, doctors, lawyers, plumbers; all walks of life that come alive on the week-end and join other Harley enthusiast for short and long rides. Learning a bit of the interior culture of such a diverse group of people was a fascinating journey for me.

Both were graduates of Mississippi State. They were, of course, maroon to the bone. They never missed a game, always had a massive tailgate party and supported any and everything State stood for. They breathed State air.

He was a president of a bank. Banker, Harley riding, chap wearing guy that touched everyone he encountered. She fashioned young minds into responsible adults. Their lives were so intermingled with each other that one seldom did anything without the other. They even bought matching Harley patches. As we say in the Deep South, Pete and re-Pete. The two of them were inseparable.

They grew up in a very small rural town, just outside of Oxford, Mississippi. Meeting in elementary school, and dated through junior and high school. Their marriage was preordained, as was the son and daughter to complete the ideal family picture.

It was in this small town, quaint in so many ways and yet so typically Southern, that I discovered who this couple was.

I set up a number of interviews in a small cafe on the town square. Half of the businesses are boarded up and at first glance it appeared to be a dying town. Later, I would learn it was like so many; a suffering town but hardly on its last leg.

The cafe was a beehive of activity. Overalls to suits kept the front door swinging. The first thing I noted was a cash register that had to date back to the twenties. It was as ornate and as large as a 1960 Buick. The black and white tile floor, the table and chairs and decor appeared to have not been changed since the sixties. It was truly the other side of the mirror, a flash back in time. It's as if the small, busy cafe had been encapsulated in a time warp, down to the soda fountain.

The wall menu had prices like a ham sandwich for a dollar, a cup of coffee for a quarter. It all felt a bit strange, like I had lost fifty years and had returned to the past. She could have walked in the door in her poodle skirt and he with his duck tails just like they did decades ago, as teenagers, madly in love.

As I sat at a small table preparing for the first interview, I noticed an elderly couple had finished their meal and left. The gent did an open palm wave to the owner as they departed. A regal lady and her well-dressed husband came in. She wiped down her glass with her kerchief and inspected the silverware. They ordered, ate and left. He also gave the owner a palm wave as the couple left. More came in and my first interviewee showed up. We talked for some time, I took notes, occasionally looking up as people came and went. There was definitely something very odd happening and I couldn't put my finger on it. I refocused on the second interview, which was a very emotional woman that worked at the bank with him.

She was very much attached, often breaking down. That was a tough interview, but very revealing. Seems her boss had sort of adopted her fatherless son, coaching his ball team and being a male figure for him. His own son was then off to college. State, of course. More customers came and went; more interviews, until I finished the last one. The cafe was a bit less busy and the owner came over and sat with me. She asked if I was hungry. I agreed to a ham sandwich. You know late at night when you get that urge for a snack and you fix a bread, mayo and ham sandwich? That's what she delivered to the table. A sandwich exactly like you would make from your refrigerator.

She spoke of the couple. She graduated high school with them and gave me the most insight as to who they were. She was considered a best friend and bridesmaid at their wedding.

Of all the interviews that day, this one was the most revealing, allowing me to actually see who they really were. A few tears, but in control, the owner told me the three of them often came to this very cafe together for malted shakes, to hear the newest songs on the jukebox and discuss their goals and future. I was right about her bouncing in the front door, poodle skirt and all. This cafe is where they met after school.

Halfway through my sandwich and busily taking notes, it occurred to me what was so bizarre...no one, not one, had stopped to pay for their meals. That huge cash register was never opened, not even once through a small herd of customers, coming and going for hours.

I asked the owner and she laughed. "OH, honey, they all come in on Saturday and settle up." I remember thinking, but this is 2013! No one does that anymore.

The couple's sorrow began with her diagnosis of breast cancer. Her treatment caused her hair to begin falling out. He shaved her head. She cried. He shaved his head and they both cried. He took off work and stayed with her every moment. Together they beat the cancer.

Eight years later the cancer came back so aggressive, there was nothing that could be done medically. He again took time off work and stayed at her bedside until she passed away. He was inconsolable.

The following month his family gathered around him to celebrate his birthday. He wasn't very attentive. A family member brought helium balloons. After everyone left, he took a felt pen and wrote a note on the balloon's streamer to his dead wife, telling her how much he missed her. He stood on his patio, said a silent prayer and released the balloon. It waffled upwards, slowly climbing until out of sight.

The next day when he went to work, the balloon with his message to her was lying at the bank's back door. Stunned, he whispered, "you got my message!"

He died two months later. What no one knew was he was diagnosed some time back with cancer. He avoided treatment so he could stay strong to care for her.

"Dear Emily" was one of the toughest and most rewarding writing assignments I've ever undertaken. It was a drain to be sure, but in the end, I knew the couple as if we had grown up on the same dusty road in that small, rural Mississippi Delta town that was frozen in time.

Standing at their tombstone, I recall thinking how remarkably ordinary they were and yet together they became something far beyond ordinary. They lived a life of extraordinary love that even death could not keep them a part.

Tomorrow is not a promise.

APRICOT CHICKEN

An easy meal for unexpected guests.

8 chicken breasts, halved
1 large jar apricot preserves
1 pkg. dried onion soup
1 bottle original Milani salad dressing

Spread chicken breast halves in a deep baking dish. Pour last three ingredients over chicken and back at 350 for one hour, covered.

Sneaking Out

I wasn't very good at explaining myself. If I knew how that lamp fell off the table or mud was tracked on a freshly mopped floor, then I would be exceptional. I'm not exceptional. I was just a kid that explored the outdoors, loved running around barefoot in shorts and a t-shirt. I didn't care if my hair was combed or if I had enough dirt in my ears to grow taters.

There were far more important matters to deal with, like catching a bull frog that had a bellow like a half grown calf. We called the illusive frog, Jeremiah. Only thing I can figure is the name Jeremiah came up in vacation Bible school, and it seemed proper to name the old bull frog. It's a singsong name that fits a singsong frog. We could only imagine that Jeremiah had to be huge, smart in age and wise enough to stay hidden. All we really knew about Jeremiah was his huge bellow. Kids claimed they got a glimpse of him, but I question their stretching the truth.

Like my older brothers that actually did go frog gigging late at night, I knew if anyone was to ever capture Jeremiah, it would have to be way beyond my bed time. The spring entertainment was lightening bugs, a mason jar and a lid with holes punched in it. If you catch enough of the gentle little critters, they would light your way. They were like the rollie-pollie bugs that wouldn't resist you and would roll up in a ball and play possum. Me and a couple of the guys had been hard at work collect lightening bugs early one evening and had a jar full. Sometimes they would light up for a few seconds and the jar would glow with their magic. One of the guys that we fondly called No Neck pulled the wings off of a lightening bug trying to figure out why the bug lit up. Wings off, the poor little creature flickered a few times and his glow of light dimmed, his life ended.

You can tell when young boys find that doorway to boredom. When you pull wings off of bugs, little minds have extended as far as they can.

At the end of No Neck's dissection, our interest was fueled and flamed by a bellow from Jeremiah. It was at that moment our plan was established. Tonight is the night that we go after Jeremiah and we had the lightening bugs to show us the way.

The three of us planned on crawling out windows or sneaking through the house, escaping the jail bars of bed time. That past Christmas I got a pair of Buck Rogers, walkie talkies. Two cans and a string would have worked better. You had to holler in the walkie talkies to be heard on the other end. Sometimes I wondered if the hollering is what we heard or if the walkie talkies actually worked. No Neck had to go without the benefit of a walkie talkie, being a third person and only two walkie talkies. He grumbled, but he was a grumbling sort of kid that never quite got satisfied with anything.

According to plan, we met at the foot of the levee at nine sharp. The evening air was chilled and the ground was cool to bare feet. Adrenalin pumping, heart pounding and anxious not to get caught, we pushed forward. No Neck brought his older brother's frog gig, I had the walkie talkies and Kirby had the jarred fireflies. The adventure had begun!

Jeremiah, right on cue, began his nightly song of matured, strong bellows. We followed the sounds towards the murky backwaters, intense and quiet. If any of us had spoken the rest would hear the shaky fear in our voice.

No Neck stepped on something that moved! He hollered out and scrambled like the Devil himself was breathing down his neck. No wait, he didn't have a neck. He ran, shouting in a blood curdling high pitched voice, SNAKE!

Kirby lowered the magic jar of lightening bugs on to a stick that shifted under No Neck's bare feet.

Shaking and scared out of our wits, we caught up to No Neck near my home. It's there that we anxiously parted company. We were all faced with breaking back into night-jail without being caught.

I opened the Mason jar and had to shake the lightening bugs to freedom then slipped back in the house. As I settled in I could hear Jeremiah off in the distance with a bellow that had a smack of laughter.

My Buck Rogers walkie talkie flashed a static sound, once then twice. Jeremiah escaped our plan that night. But Kirby's jailers caught him trying to break into his nightly cell.

In the silence of the night, after the clicking of the walkie talkie had stopped and Jeremiah had finished his nightly song, my mind wandered back to vacation Bible school and the voice of the young teenager overseeing our class. It was his wisdom that came to mind.

Don't expect good when you know you are doing something wrong. Years later, as an adult, I am reminded and laugh of that night when the singer sings:

"Jeremiah was a bull frog."

CHUCK ROAST

Simple but delicious.

1 pkg. onion soup mix
1 can mushroom soup

Mix and pour over 1 ½ lb. roast. Cover with foil and bake in oven for two hours at 350
The larger the roast, the longer the cook time.
Quick and easy.

Toys and Trials

Hula hoop. Now there was a fairly simple idea that made millions. Although it wasn't considered manly, at nine years old, being manly is still a few years out. And besides, who could resist? I tried it. What was amazing was the girls that could get ten or fifteen of those bad boys going at once. It was great to watch but not something just anyone could do. Or, maybe it was just me. I had way too much trouble with just one. Five minutes of trying and I was done.

Now my sisters could walk around the house with the silly plastic circle around their waist, do their chores and never give it a second thought. I suppose it was a girl fad and I was proof positive that guys just aren't meant to hula hoop. Try it, yes...go down in flames quickly and move on to the marble game already in progress.

Our front yard on Poplar Street had no grass. Seriously, it was as bald as Uncle Henry. It's hard to grow grass in total shade. The massive oak tree in our front yard had enough lumber to build a castle and blocked the sun. With the shade of the tree and kids constantly playing there, grass didn't have a chance. We didn't mind that there wasn't any grass, in fact, we were kind of happy about it. It's hard to play marbles in the grass.

If you've seen powdery sandy loam before, then you can get a glimpse of why our front yard became the mecca for marble shooters. It was close to a fine sandy beach, maybe with some dusty flour added in and was perfect for drawing a ring with an index finger. You could build up a powdery mound to rest your hand on for those down-hard killer shots.

Marbles was my game, at least in my own mind. That sort of thinking kept my marble bag to a low count and plenty trips to Ben Franklin's dime store for additional fire power. Blue cat-eyes seemed to be my lucky marble. Most guys back then had a lucky marble. If it wasn't lucky, it was for sure their favorite. Losing my favorite marble was kind of tough. It was even worse losing your lucky blue cat-eye marble, which I did way too often.

I can clearly remember the day that my dad who worked at the Gypsum Mill brought home some small bearings. They were about the size of a regular marble only they were stainless steel. You pop a glass marble with one of those steelies and your marble bag population grew quick. We had a monopoly on steelies and you can bet one never-ever loses a steelie, unless...

I was content knocking off as many marbles as I could and was especially happy when I busted someone's favorite marble out of the ring. There was a bit of devil in me in slowly dropping their favorite marble into my leather bag. Their anguished face was my reward. I believed in Karma back then, and still do. You are going to get back just what you put out. What that meant was, I had a lot of blue-eyes about to find a new home. Actually, they found a new marble bag to live in...In the same home!

My brother, two years older, figured out the more he shot with a heavy steelie, the stronger his thumb muscle got. Sort of like lifting weights for your thumbs. Every time I played him, we ended our game with his full marble bag and mine empty, including my steelies. Karma gave me a payback kiss. Something I've never quite got about Karma. How can you win without a touch, at least a little delight in someone else losing?

It's the delight that gets a red mark by your name and Karma comes to collect. There's a middle ground I'm sure. I just never found it.

After losing all of my marbles and no Ben Franklin money in my pocket, I was left to the sole sport of yo-yoing. Got fairly good at around the world and walking the dog, but the really fancy tricks got lost between the ring finger, my brain and the plastic yo-yo. Maybe the yo-yo was kind of like the hula hoop. Maybe it takes someone special to do all the really cool tricks.

One older brother had a fancy yellow plastic yo-yo that had flickering, internal lights. He was really good at it and when he added in the light show, his act was mesmerizing. (That's a dollar word for hypnotizing). He had that snap to every move and a return that was so cool. He was like an Olympic star, perfect timing, perfect moves with the grace of a cat, always landing on their feet.

I decided it wasn't a good time for me. My sisters showed me up on the hula hoop, one brother outshined me in the marble ring and another brother smoked me with his incredible yo-yo act.

Sometimes it wasn't fun being the youngest.

What my older siblings never knew was Mom slipped me extra desserts.

She kept my world balanced.

RIBS

Fast and easy barbecued ribs

1 c. water
4 lbs. spare ribs cut into serving pieces

Place water and ribs in a slow cooker. Turn to low heat and cover. Cook 8 hours. Drain ribs and place in a broiling pan. Brush both sides with Sweet Baby Ray's BBQ sauces. Broil at 350 for 15-20 minutes or until well browned.

Look Deeper

Greenville, Mississippi, is not a big flashy town. Like any sought after jewel worth digging for, she has treasures and secrets that usually remain within the hometown family. Doe's Eat Place is another matter. Working at the local airport I encountered many well-heeled travelers that flew to Greenville for one reason; a delectable steak like no other. Some secret treasures can't be hidden, especially once the word gets out. It's kind of sad that the steak hungry didn't search beyond their appetite and discover some of the other traditions and treasures that were less obvious, like the home town folk that made you feel like family.

In the fourth grade at Susie P. Trigg, Mrs. Black encouraged me to write more. She was impressed with a short essay that I had written. Her voice and encouragement repeated itself throughout high school and college. But, life happens. Job, family, responsibilities all seem to take one into other directions. Writing offered very little money, if any, and was time consuming.

Looking back, that time was better spent supporting and raising a family and pursuing and nurturing the next generation's aspirations. But, as in most lives, there are unexpected hard turns that change the flow and direction one thinks is their preordained route on this earth. The airline had moved from what was once a small family, into a larger, less familiar work place. That followed with more mergers, becoming one of the largest airlines on earth. The world was changing and the changes were not always good changes. Our patchwork, over-merged, behemoth airline lost that small town, friendly, one on one personal customer service and family values. The qualities that kept me excited and motivated warped into a corporate cash cow, no longer recognizable to a small town guy that grew up in an environment of caring, family oriented, personable service that honored their customers and employees.

To put a fine point on it, and to quote a twenty-three year old Human Resource employee, just out of college and on the airline payroll less than six months," if you believe this company is your future, you've become a dinosaur." After thirty-seven dedicated, wonderful years I knew the time had come for a drastic change. This dinosaur had some serious pondering to do. The multi-million dollar operation I ran with seventy-five employees that looked to me for leadership was losing the shine. I was no longer excited about going to work or hyped about whatever project of development I was engaged in. The last thing I wanted to become was someone hanging on; living in another era. It was time to take advantage of an early-out retirement program. I knew I could handle another ten or twelve years and retire at normal retirement age. But, I also knew that happiness outweighed running out the clock. I took the early out and took steps to begin another career, writing. Maybe, my fourth grade teacher, Mrs. Black, was right. What I discovered is, I can create worlds, people and circumstances uninhibited with cash cows or corporate greed influencing me. Rather, it is my influence on them. I had the newly found power of reaching back to tight knit families and rural towns where people moved slower, taking time to smell an oncoming rain.

Life went from complicated to simple. It's the simple where I began. It's a way of life that Greenville offered in my formative years. To me, it's the very essence of who we are and how we became who we are. It's my aim to find that time and place when life meant something special. When people were sensitive towards each other and the twenty-four hour news had not so removed us from the realities that we didn't hurt when others hurt.

I've lived the corporate life, chasing after excellence, developing nothing into something. The endless challenges were stimulating and exciting. I am grateful to the airline and all that it provided for me and my family. But, my wife no longer has to reach over and slow my eating hand. I'm no longer running in place with my mind racing to the next airline challenge.

Rather, I'm doing something that has been said one can't do, "It's impossible. You cannot go home." However, if only for a few minutes, I believe you can go home. It's a journey worthwhile. Deep within a visit back home you find out who you are and what really matters. You hurt to hear that another high school classmate has passed on. You feel something when you discover one of your long ago friends is terminally ill. There's anger discovering the guy you once competed with in a sixth grade spelling bee was senselessly beaten by thugs for twelve dollars.

The key word, at least for me, is FEEL. It's something we were taught, something we witnessed through family and friends. We care enough to feel something when others hurt. And, we celebrate their celebrations. It's what connects us to each other. When we lose the ability to feel, we become the corporate cash cow, we become the twenty-four hour news that desensitizes us to other's pain. We become lost and disconnected.

In my mind's eye, I go back to Greenville and attempt to put my search into words. It's between those words that I hope to stir your own memories and remind you of a place and time when the greatest generation taught us the basic values of caring and feeling. They taught us we can do the impossible.

Be the best of what your parents taught you.

PEA PICKING CAKE

1 pkg. Duncan Hines yellow butter cake mix
1 small can of mandarin oranges
4 eggs
½ c. Wesson oil (any quality cooking oil will do)

Combine and beat ingredients together until well mixed.
Pour into 2 greased cake pans and bake 25 minutes at 350.

ICING

1 large container Cool Whip
1 large can crushed pineapple
1 small pkg. vanilla custard Jell-O pudding mix

Combine pineapple with Jell-O pudding mix and fold in Cool
Whip. Spread over cake and refrigerate overnight.

Tubing

Summer of 1960, I was eleven, no wait I would have been eleven and a half. That almighty half-thing pushed me closer to becoming a fine young man, rather than the gangling, all knees and elbows, awkward child that I so obviously was.

It was a bizarre time. I went from one day sporting my cap guns and plastic spurs to the next day spending hours in front of a mirror combing my hair in every direction, in an earnest quest for the man-style of the day.

My oldest brother was the coolest guy ever, with his duck tails and black leather jacket. My sister laid her head on the ironing board while a friend actually ironed her hair straight. I can tell you the smell of burning hair lingers way longer than an angered skunk.

Hair was a big thing back then. It defined who you were. I had a lot of trouble finding out who I was between all the hair parting and flip flopping between youth and teen. One day I would spend my time humming into a fan to hear my childish "echo" and the next, I was wearing long pants and shoes.

Thinking back, I suppose since we didn't have much money and a lot of time on our hands, vanity kept our backs straight. Mother was an understanding woman that gave us a lot of room to experiment and find out exactly who we were, in our own immature way. What I do not remember is her offering the advice that vanity can and often does backfire causing one to dig out the cap guns and plastic spurs and retreat back into the world of carefree childhood.

No matter where we were on the growing up spectrum, manners were taught and expected. In case you've forgotten, allow me to remind you.

At age eleven and a half, manners are often set aside to explore just how stupid one can be by pushing known parameters and looking for new forbidden freedoms.

Vanity has a twin brother and that twin travels under the name of Lying. It's stretching the truth, overstating, and purposely hiding what is accurate and correct. All of which carries a punishment far beyond forgetting manners. At the age of back and forth, child today, young man the next; the ability to hide the truth and amplify that which will advance the belief of being more than you are, came to visit me one hot day that summer.

We had a neighbor that collectively, it was decided had to be rich. He always drove a new car, was well dressed and had two daughters that were drop dead gorgeous. Not a surprise when you see him and his wife together. They looked like Mister and Miss Greenville High, twenty years later. The perfect, star quarterback married to the beautiful head cheerleader. Of course, their kids would be stunning.

What convinced us of his wealth was his dynamic speed boat. Sleek, shiny and could surely out run the wind. It's the best use of fiberglass known to mankind, short of the invincible Corvette. His generous invitation to join him and his family on the speed boat for an afternoon of tubing and skiing was an offer that I couldn't refuse.

When asked if I knew how to "tube", the twin brother to vanity, LYING, kicked in. I left no doubt that I was the tubing champion of the Greater South. Truth? I'd never seen a tube or had any idea of what tubing is. I'd never even been on a boat. All I knew was, I was eight feet tall and bullet proof and must have parted my hair just the right way to get the invitation.

On the ride out to deeper water on Lake Ferguson, the two daughters told me the story of a water skier that saw a mangle of barbed wire floating in the water. He signaled the boat that he was going to remove the dangerous barbed wire from the water and dropped the ski rope near the mangled mess. As it turns out, it wasn't barbed wire as he thought, but a boiling heap of water moccasins. That story still gives me the willies.

Their dad, being the cultured gentleman that he was, offered to let me have the first ride on the tube. That's when I realized what a tube was. As I eased into the water my eyes darted around for barbed wire. I knew no matter what, I was hanging on to that rope! I was bullet proof, not snake proof.

As I eased into the tube, he waited for my thumbs up...a sign I didn't know I was supposed to flash. The daughters gave me a thumbs up, so I flashed one back...that's when the tube slowly started to move forward. I remember thinking; this is a piece of cake. What I didn't know was I was about to have the whole cake come crashing down on me.

He sped up and made a large sweeping turn. Peachy keen! I'm holding my own, keeping a sharp eye out for barbed wire and waving to the beautiful daughters. One hand, white knuckled, holding on to the rope that tethered me to the boat.

I was loving the speed and the wind blowing in my face and then I watched the boat go by me, almost in slow motion. How can he be pulling me when we are beside each other? It didn't take but a moment before the rope took the shortest distance. Speed times parallel, equals a massive, snatching, turn-about with the force of the Blue Angels at takeoff. Here comes Karma.

I vaguely remember my entire body being snatched into the Twilight Zone. My life flashed before me. All eleven and one half years, went tumbling in the air, free of the tube, and free of the rope. All life lines irreversibly removed. If I don't die on impact, surely the barbed wire will get me. Unless someone has told you, you really aren't familiar with gentle water becoming concrete at that rate of speed. Having the eight foot tall and bullet proof vanity that day, had me doing mid-air flips before crashing into the murky water. I knew my time had come. Life stopped at the end of a tubing rope. Justice found its reward and the balance of good and evil restored.

My entire body ached and burned. I could hear the boat's motor, so I knew I must still be alive. It was then, at that very moment, I remembered I had just earned my Minnow patch at the YMCA. Minnows took great pride in the fact that they had learned to keep their head above water and at best dog paddle a very short distance. Swimming wasn't one of my greater accomplishments. Thank goodness for the belt lifesaver my neighbor insisted I wear. It was the law. A law introduced to offset vanity, I'm sure.

Later, after I was fished out of the water, the daughters told me they counted three flips before I hit the water. They smiled, so I thought maybe three mid-air flips was cool. I'm still not sure how I accomplished a belly flop and a back flop on the same water entry, but I'll leave that up to a physics class to figure out. I hid my pain as I watched the daughters ride the tube. They were seasoned travelers across the muddied waters of Lake Ferguson.

Later, I tried not to limp when they dropped me off at my home. It was all quite an adventure that prepared me to return to my plastic spurs, cap guns and a tall glass of ice cold red, Kool-Aid. I'll find the "man" way to part my hair another day.

That night in bed, aching, I replayed the day and the circumstances that got me in the quagmire. I remember promising myself I would never lie again. It's a promise that has been broken over and over. The twins, Vanity and Lying, challenge and remind me that the truth will surface, even without a lifebelt.

The best we can hope for is life's surface doesn't have barbed wire.

FRENCH COCONUT PIE

3 eggs beaten well
1 ½ c. sugar
1 stick margarine
1 c. shredded coconut
1 tbsp. vinegar
1 tsp. vanilla flavoring

Combine ingredients and pour into an unbaked pie shell and bake for 1 hour at 350.

Great Dame

We are what we are exposed to. We become something more and at times something less as people move in and out of our lives.

As a writer, it becomes a sixth sense to pay attention to details. It is the details that when added up, becomes that person. Some are colorful; some are less exciting, while others seem to have the world by the tail with a Midas result. I want to tell you about one colorful person I met.

While on assignment I was scheduled to meet with an elderly person to interview her about her great nephew. The story I was writing focused on him. The family member that arranged the interview failed to mention that the person I was to interview walked straight out of a Civil War drama. Pay attention to the details.

After driving through Oxford, Mississippi, I knew I was getting close. My GPS showed their address twelve miles from where I sat at the moment.

As I got closer, "Ethel", the robotic GPS voice, told me to turn left and arrive at my destination. Impossible! She's led me astray. This can't be where I am headed. Before me was a manor; a plantation home that stood with twenty massive, white pillars; each four feet in diameter. A massive, elaborate home front that smacked of Twelve Oaks from "Gone with the Wind."

"Ethel" and I bantered back and forth. I recycled the GPS and re-entered the address. I was exactly where I was supposed to be. The address and "Ethel" matched. I pulled into the driveway, wider than I-55, which led up to one of the most impressive, stunning homes I've ever been within walking distance of. It was Graceland on steroids.

I hesitantly parked and slowly walked to the front porch, knowing "Ethel" was having her fun with me. I could smell the mint juleps and hear the ice clanking in fine crystal. A grand ball could be held on the front porch. Gray uniform soldiers toast the genteel, hooped dressed, fine ladies. If a person could, in today's times, walk onto a movie set of "Gone with the Wind" this would be the place. I was literally in the middle of nowhere and had truly stepped into the Twilight Zone; back into an era of when cotton was king.

I lifted the large, heavy brass knocker and let it fall back against the huge wooden front door. Seconds later, the massive door swung open and a frail looking, small lady stood before me. She couldn't have been more than eighty pounds, perfectly coiffured, manicured and dressed to the nines. She had a pleasant, albeit wrinkled face, with light make up befitting a woman in her eighties.

With a grand gesture of inviting one in, she slightly bowed with a sweeping arm, extending the courtesy to walk on hallowed ground. I was obviously stunned. Her youthful voice, coated in Confederacy and dripped of old money said, "I was expecting you, kind sir. Please enter."

Remember the details? Her voice was most striking. The Aristocratic Southern dialect was alive and well. She represented the upper-most crust of Southern society dating back to Robert E Lee.

As I entered she once again with a slight bow and sweeping arm directed me beyond the foyer and into a room just off of the grand living room. There on a desk that Jefferson Davis himself could have used, was a large open book. Above the book was a large white feathered pen.

"Everyone, whom enters, must sign my guest book," dripped slowly from her mouth.

The only guest books I've ever signed were at weddings and funerals. I've never held a quill in my life. Leaning slightly forward, I went to write my name and noticed two names up was the signature of the present Governor of Mississippi. I'm not easily impressed but that sort of rocked my boat a little bit.

I smiled at this gracious creature after signing her visitor's book and was led through an incredible journey of touring the massive, endless mansion. At this point I'm not sure if she is maybe a curator occupying the home and playing the role of long-gone Aristocracy, to the level of Oscar winner or the actual owner of this Rod Serling, Twilight Zone Confederate Plantation Estate.

After the lengthy, seemingly endless tour and after climbing three flights of stairs, we observed the "writing room" that was occupied by her father's, father. It was then that I realized she wasn't a curator. She was a generational owner that loved her home as well as all of the era pieces of magnificent furniture. Each room, she proudly showed me, had a ceiling centerpiece chandelier that to my estimation, was priceless. This little bundle of endless energy guided me back down the winding staircase, holding onto the beautiful, ornate, banister. This led to the most modern part of the house, the kitchen, which obviously was added on in more modern times.

I asked if the home was a historical landmark. Her left hand gently rested against her kind, porcelain face and said, "Lord, yes!" Years ago her grandfather had attended to such matters.

There in her kitchen I was served high tea in a dainty cup that held not much more than a whisper of hot tea. The only high tea I have ever had, was with my three year old granddaughters. Give me a mason jar packed with ice and sweet tea and I'm good. High tea, unless it's on the pretend scale with someone three feet tall that fills your cup with air, isn't my cup of... Okay, I guess you saw that coming.

Over and hour after I arrived, we finally settled down to my purpose, which was to interview her about her great nephew, the topic of my current assignment. Crumpets offered and politely declined, she began her stories related to her grandnephew. He was her student back when she taught school. In fact she was teacher to the Mayor, Chief of Police, Fire Chief and so on. I nearly fell out of my chair when she told me in her enchanting genteel, Southern voice heavy laden of old money that when the negras invaded her then all white school, she resigned.

Again, stepping back in time, it was a dialogue that only Rod Serling could write for one of his Twilight Zone episodes. We heard of the grandeur, we read about it, seen pictures of it, but to actually experience it first hand, was something I will never forget.

She was a Grand Dame of the Old South; a throwback to a time when people lived their lives separated by color and money. On that day during my time with her, I began to realize that I lived the last breath of that era when judgment fell on color. Our small town that I grew up in was segregated. What did we know? We were kids and hardly responsible for the past.

She had given me a tour not only of her magnificent home but a history lesson of my beloved South when cotton was king and money spoke in a loud voice.

We truly are a combination of all the people that we meet throughout our lives. Greenville, Mississippi provided an endless parade of magnificent people that enriched lives with their wisdom and leadership. As I grow older and see more and more of the world, I better understand that not all small towns had that wisdom and just how fortunate we were to have been at the right place with the right people, at the right time.

We learn from everyone we meet. From Grand Dame of the South to the plumber that keeps the home flow in shape. The trick, at least for me, is to pay attention to the details. People speak who they are, but only when we listen do we understand.

May your own details reflect the person you would love to meet.

Giddy Up!

Y'all remember Bob Porter, my giddy up buddy that never questions my hair brain ideas? He saddles up and is ready for whatever comes.

Friends like Bob are hard to find and even harder to keep, especially if you have more than a few dumb ideas and are willing to lay out a plan of action. Bob, Bless him, never not once, ever questioned whatever strange or bizarre idea I had cooked up.

I have never had any lessons, direction or any formal training for painting on canvas. I know what looks good. I know what colors appeal and I know what subjects have some attraction. At least that's what I thought. And in my mind, I'm as perfect as any human. So, off we go to the craft store. Bob bought exactly everything I bought; canvases, paintbrushes, paint and an official plastic palette. We were pumped and ready to put our art on canvas for posterity.

Bob came over, got set up and we began painting. Remember, no experience, no guidance, nothing more than sheer desire. After we had seven or eight pictures, each, I decided we were ready to have our own show. Laugh, its okay. Brazen as I am, I'll understand. No one in Greenville was willing to loan their art gallery to us. They never looked at our paintings and I can only assume after they met and spoke with us, they realized we were both giddy up sort of guys and never stopped to learn the basics.

I was offended the first time someone called my painting primitive. Little did I know that was a compliment and an area of art that requires some talent for it to be good. Primitive describes your subject matter, which is of course, rural Southern cotton fields, shacks and ancient barns.

Undaunted, my plan B was to start "showing" at arts and craft events. This ended up being quite a learning curve. It was an immediate education on how the craft world operates. You pay rental for a space and you have to have your own presentation materials. For us, that meant we needed bi-fold vented doors to hang our art work on. We needed folding tables, a cash box and some folding chairs. The investment was growing and the income at that point, was exactly zero. So far, the money is going in the wrong direction; out of our pockets instead of in. Bob never flinched. He ponied up his half and we pushed forward. As it turned out we didn't need a cash box. When you haven't collected any cash, you certainly don't need the box.

I booked our first "show" in Dumas, Arkansas. It was obvious our home town was not ready for our talent.

Folks from Dumas are candid. They are refreshingly honest, blunt and hard to hood wink. Early that first morning the first guy that walked up to our booth was an older farmer, rough sewn and terribly honest. My got ego bruised. I didn't prepare for his unvarnished lack of appreciation of mine or Bob's work. We dusted off that guy with a "What does he know?" I told Bob we needed to rearrange our display. That was the problem. We didn't have our canvases properly displayed. In the next few hours, the old farmer's estimation was repeated a number of times, usually by some small and probably otherwise nice ladies that simply had no filter on their comments.

It's about that time that Bob and I decided Arkansas maybe wasn't the right market for our artwork. The next arts and craft show I booked was in Cleveland, Mississippi. They were our people, our audience. We were fairly deep into the investment at this point and we were past the point of needing profit, if for nothing else, to help cover our present expenses. Our cash box remained empty. Dry. Barren.

As the sun beat down on our tent and the sunlight reflected on our canvases, the passer-by crowd didn't stop to look. We were simply passed up. Again, I figured the problem was the way we had our artwork displayed. As I feverishly rearranged the canvases, a little girl, maybe twelve or so came up to me and asked if I could help her.

It wasn't like business was booming, so I stopped to see what it was that she wanted. Her dad is a carpenter. Okay, I got that. At least he wasn't like the Arkansas farmer that couldn't stop laughing at our artwork. The little girl handed me a used circular saw blade and told me her dad collected anything that had Coke Cola on it. She thought maybe a barn with a coke sign on the barn's side would please her dad, who was about to celebrate a birthday.

I asked her to come back in about an hour and I would have her Coke barn painted for her at the price of five dollars. It took me a few minutes to get the feel for a painting so small but once I got started, it all begun to fall into place. A young woman stopped at our table and completely skipped over the canvases and admired the barn I was painting on a saw blade. She ordered six of them.

I sent Bob to the nearest hardware store to buy saw blades and some flat black for a background. Giddy up. Bob never questioned the odd request.

Before Bob got back I had twenty orders for Coke barns on a saw blade. We spent the rest of that day catching up with demand and taking more orders. Bob paid three dollars for each saw blade, but at least we had some income, as small as it was. We made money!

When we got back to Greenville, it occurred to me that we had a saw blade factory and I bet Nicholson File had rejects that we could buy for far less than three bucks a pop. With some negotiations, we managed to get an unlimited supply of various saw blades for about a nickel each. We pushed up the price to seven dollars and we sold more than we could paint. It's then that I learned how to line up eight blades and paint grass and sky all at once. Bob took a look and giddy up, he did the same thing. We still couldn't keep up with the demand. Every show we went to we sold out and took orders to be mailed. The canvases never sold. We left them home after the second show and from then on, only brought saw blades with us.

Then it happened. Greenville caught on. We showed at a small craft show that was a sidewalk affair down by Stein Mart, at the foot of the levee. We sold out and took orders.

I never went to another show without at least one hundred already painted blades. We continued to sell out for the next seven years, until my airline, my day job, pulled up roots and moved away from Greenville.

I tell this story for a reason beyond seeking out a giddy up buddy like Bob; although everyone should be so lucky to have a friend like Bob. It doesn't matter if convention tells us that we aren't smart enough, trained enough or experienced enough, when we set our minds to something, no matter how off the wall it may seem to be, we have that inner strength that is inherent from the Mississippi Delta, do or die.

We don't listen to naysayers. We follow our dream. Look at the farmers that have become successful and the pioneers that started up tow boat companies, or a guy that made and remade tamales until they were perfect. You know they all heard that what they were trying would fail. You know they all had an Arkansas farmer tell them their art stunk, but they did it anyway.

Look at all of the successful people that got their start in Greenville. They had their eyes on the prize and went deaf to the naysayers. Think about the musicians that were told they couldn't play music and today, those untalented people are literally all over the world as successful musicians. Writers of all stripes and sorts that now have an international audience.

Fate has a way with people that refuse to let their dreams die. I firmly believe Fate smiles on people with desires so deep within their soul, they don't know what it means to give up.

Babe Ruth had more hits than any other ballplayer of his time. He also held the record for strike outs.

No one pays any attention to the strike outs. Giddy up!

Be Honest

Kick the can. It was a late evening summer game that occupied the neighborhood kids.

Poplar and Alexander hosted a number of families, usually large families with a lot of kids that were roughly the same age. Most of us avoided prison.

There was one family, obviously fairly new to our neighborhood, from Germany. Their accent was thick-tongued, awkward and their English poor. They had only one child and if she were the measuring stick for having children, there would have been fewer kids in the world. Wilma surely had the devil whispering in her ear constantly. Kids don't cheat at kick the can. Wilma is the only kid I know that did.

Although that wasn't her only vice, it did separate her from the rest of us. We tried to be welcoming and accept her as one of our own but when a kid in our neighborhood is proven to be a liar and or a cheat, that kid was forever cut from the herd. Wilma didn't stay within the herd for long. After a game or two of kick the can and a few other incidents that proved her character flawed, she became an outcast. She became an instant loner, black-balled.

We would walk the levee and behind stores on Washington Avenue in search of empty Coke and Pepsi bottles. The purpose was to collect the deposit money on the bottles and earn enough to go to the Paramount. Wilma was left out of those adventures. Like the time we found an unopened case of typewriter ribbons. They were obviously stolen and hidden in the trash dump, the very place we searched for empty cola bottles.

The incident raised a big stink with the local policemen thinking that we had stolen the typewriter ribbons and then had second thoughts about giving them back. We may have been poor, a bit wild, and even reckless, but stealing wasn't what we did. Since the owner's name was printed on the box we returned it to him. He regained his stock and was grateful. He funded a trip to the movies with popcorn for all four of us. We did a good deed and were rewarded for it. That's how things are supposed to work. Not that you expect to get a reward for a good deed, but it's always nice when it happens that way.

When you do bad things, you get the consequences. That's how that works, too. Although in today's Government, the proven golden rule principle has most certainly morphed into something that appears to be reversed and backwards from guiding principles that every kid, on every block, in every city, in America should know and embrace. It's hard for kids to learn how to be good when adults set the example and do bad.

Wilma became a terror as time moved forward and she was left out of everything. She didn't recognize that bad begets bad. Maybe there was a language problem, or maybe within the walls of her home, all she saw was bad. Whatever the reason, this small version of a she-devil had her fill one afternoon and picked up a sharp edge rock that found its way to my forehead, splitting it open and leaving a large gash.

Before I made it back to my home, I was almost blinded by the flowing blood, now covering my face. Anyone that has experienced a head injury knows that there's always a scary amount of blood.

My dad without any hesitation immediately grabbed me up and put me on his handlebars of his bicycle and drove me to

Dr. Acree's office for stitches. The four stitches in the shaved area looked a lot worse than it was.

As a result, with no apology from Wilma or her parents, they moved that night. We never heard from them again.

While I am destined to have that scar the rest of my life, I couldn't help but wonder what happened to Wilma. Maybe she went on to become a famous movie star or is serving time at Parchman. Wherever she may be, Wilma brought something sinister to our neighborhood. It was an evil that we hadn't seen before or since. We learned from her that there are kids that cheat at kick the can and do even worse. That's the kids we were taught to avoid.

Now I believe in being inclusive. Everyone should be given a chance. But if they blow it, if they prove themselves to be cut from a different cloth, then they become the kids our parents always told us to stay away from.

Kids in our neighborhood didn't come from wealthy families, but what we did have was a great set of morals. Being poor didn't mean you were corrupt. We didn't cheat. We didn't lie (unless a pending spanking was involved and then we would lie a blue streak), but we didn't set out to be mean. We understood the Ten Commandments and respected adults. We weren't perfect but we didn't do demonic stuff. Well, except Buster. He tied two cats' tails together and threw them over Miss Mabel's clothesline. They would have killed each other if Miss Mable's son hadn't swatted them off the clothesline with a broom. Lucky, when the cats hit the ground the old shoe string Buster used to tie the tails together broke.

Buster got his GED at Parchman Prison. You know what they say about kids that are cruel to animals. He went on to bigger and more serious things that landed him time in the big house. He was one of only a very few from our neighborhood that ended up at a house of correction.

Justice finds its own rewards in its own time, and it's not always in a court of law. Its name is Karma and Karma will not be denied. You put out bad, you can bet Karma will hunt you down.

It's in a simple game of kick the can that you discover a kid's moral compass. For us, there were plenty of kids that knew the difference in right and wrong. Maybe we didn't dress in the day's high fashions and maybe didn't drive a Mercedes convertible, but we knew right from wrong and didn't allow our meager beginnings to draw us away from the principles our parents instilled in us. It's those times that we could have cheated and didn't, that made us strong for the future.

Having money, fine clothes and a sporty car, doesn't make you a better person. It's what inside you that counts, even when you play kick the can.

Playing by the rules is a lifelong lesson. Get started early.

Live the Golden Rule

The last few days of heavy rain has kept me inside. With the thunder bumpers and lightening, you never know when Mother Nature may put you in the dark.

Your choices are to fight the weather and complain or you can have what I call reflective moments. This is when you allow your mind to sort out whatever seems to dominate at the time.

There's always something to think about and for that, we should be grateful. Imagine for a moment that life is perfect. We'd worry about whatever is about to happen and not enjoy the moment of perfect. I'm not sure about other folks but perfect doesn't happen for me very often. Maybe I'm a worrier. Or, maybe I'm a realist. We know perfect moments are few and far between but I simply do not want them to end.

The most perfect, imperfect Easter that comes to mind is when I was seven or eight years old. The weather was changing so fast and so often that we didn't know if it was going to snow or turn into heavy rains. Either way, you can't hunt Easter eggs in crappy weather. Yes, a snow around Easter is likely. It's not so unusual that folks in the Delta know of the probability. A short sleeve Christmas and a blinding snow Easter has happened more than once.

Dad was an innovator, a motivator and all round happy guy that didn't allow weather or other circumstances dampen his outlook. I've wondered why I didn't inherit that incredible trait from him. I have to catch myself while in a moment of perfect, relax, and just live in that moment. I have to remind myself to take in my surrounding and breathe in the joy of perfect. Those moments are fleeting at best and if you are worrying about later, you aren't enjoying the now. My dad was a master of the now.

Dark skies, rumbling thunder and flashes of light mixed with bitter cold, I remember looking out my bedroom window, miserable at the thought that the highly anticipated Easter egg hunt would be cancelled.

That morning the eight of us sat at the kitchen table and dyed eggs. We competed to see who could dip, double dip, triple dip and mix colors to come out with the most impressive, most unusual egg. Even the joy and competition didn't remove the blue of the weather from me. I wasn't in the perfect moment of family fun. With the white wax crayon, I wrote "blah" on the egg I dyed. "Blah" glowed against the dark blue dyed egg.

We ate lunch with Dad at the head of the table. He told his six kids that the weather wasn't going to stop our Easter. He sent us to my older brother's bedroom, no peeking, while he and Mom hid Easter eggs throughout the house. An indoor Easter egg hunt? It was a perfect moment that I couldn't believe in. It was a moment that seemed too farfetched to be real. But I did as I was told and went into the bedroom with my siblings.

Soon, dad came to the bedroom door and said the classic get on your mark, get set, "GO!" The treasure hunt began, releasing six anxious siblings, scrambling to find not only Easter eggs but the ultimate "golden egg". The golden egg always had a five dollar bill in it. At age seven, five dollars was like a million dollars.

What seemed impossible, turned into kids laughing, digging under the couch, leaning chairs back and happily rearranging the furniture all in search of the illusive golden egg.

As the frantic pace lessened and the counted three dozen eggs were found, the golden egg remained missing. The silver egg with two dollars in it was found by one brother that had a satisfying grin ear to ear. But, the pressing question was, where is the golden egg?

Mom and Dad always hid exactly three dozen eggs and two special eggs. We had to keep count because nothing you can imagine smells worse than a decaying egg. Back then, we actually used real eggs, except the two very special eggs that had money in them. The family tradition began after one Easter Dad had bought Mom a very special Easter candy treat that came in the two large plastic eggs. The golden egg was gold. The silver egg, as we called it, was a pale blue.

With the pale blue egg found and all of the other Easter eggs found the real hunt became serious as the six of us elbowed our way from this spot to that in hopes of striking it rich.

I suppose maybe because I was the youngest, or maybe because Dad sensed that dark and stormy weather caused me to be a bit dark and stormy he tilted his head towards the toaster on the kitchen counter. He didn't outright point or say anything but his eyes danced and glistened and that wonderful understanding smile told me to look behind the toaster.

There was joy and excitement as I held the big dollar egg up high in the air and my siblings moaned. My feet and spirits lifted when I hollered, "I found it!"

With the Easter egg hunt over and all the anticipation and excitement subsided, I pondered on how to spend my fortune. I was rich. The world was mine for the buying. Money was tight. It always is in a big family. I sat at my bedroom window staring out at the bleak weather while my brothers and sisters did the egg fight. One cracks his egg against another's. The winner's egg didn't crack. I never did master what my oldest brother knew. He always won and I ate my boiled egg in defeat.

Missing out on the egg fights and staring out into the bleak weather is when it occurred to me that Dad allowed me to find the golden egg. I wondered why. There are five other kids that would have been just as excited, just as happy to have been the one to find the golden egg. It was then, at seven years old I saw a bit of what joy and giving is all about. Dad suspected, maybe he knew, I'm not sure, but that night at the dinner table I announced how I intended to spend my newly found fortune.

It cost a quarter to go to the Paramount. The Roy Rogers cowboy hat that I wanted was a buck and a quarter. It was my decision to buy the cowboy hat and take all eight of us to the movies. My siblings were happy with the decision. Dad gave me his knowing smile. It was a perfect moment.

Maybe I did inherit Dad's sense of now. Maybe it's been there all along. I do know that dark and stormy weather pulls me down. Maybe that's a natural reaction that most people encounter. The trick, at least for me, is to get past the darkness of the moment and seek out the perfect. It's when we are in those perfect moments that we become the person we are meant to be.

There's a battle every dusk when the light fights to stay alive as the darkness takes over. The good news is that battle has no permanent winner.

Moments are precious. Embrace the perfect.

Ride if You Dare

One of the essentials for a Greenville childhood was cardboard boxes. Living a block off of Washington Avenue made it easy to rummage behind all of the stores for the perfect cardboard box, depending on which adventure we were on that day.

Large appliance boxes were perfect for building forts and protecting us from the onslaught of chinaberries or dirt clod wars. The only drawback was if we got a good rain, our fort would melt to a flat heap of uselessness.

On other days, for other adventures, the perfect box usually came from Ben C. Penn's. The size was ideal for splitting open, making it flat, creating a sled of sorts, to ride down the levee.

The town side of the levee has a slight angled berm that flows into a second berm with a much tamer slant. The ride from the top of the levee was fantastic for the first berm but when meeting the second berm the ride slowed, usually to a stop.

Now on the water side of the levee, life and cardboard moved faster because there was a critical decline with no berm breaks. It was literally a sheer angle that once you got started on the slide downward you went faster the further you traveled. Standing at the top of the levee with a running start and a good faith leap head first, like a dive off the high diving board at the Bobby Henry swimming pool, you went head first at a speed that made it difficult to remain on the cardboard. Eating grass was a bonus. The momentum plus the critical angle was more than a challenge to not slide off the cardboard and be introduced to some lasting grass burns.

It didn't take long to recognize the town side was a much tamer ride and the water side of the levee was an unpredictable wild ride that got the adrenalin pumping and heart pounding. If you could keep the cardboard underneath you and balance yourself just so, you could make it all the way to the bottom of the levee. Congratulations, you earned bragging rights for the day! Truthfully, you could count yourself lucky if you survived the ride. The water side was as close as we could get to a homemade carnival ride.

Twice a year, early spring, at school's summer break and late fall, we had a traveling carnival come to Greenville. I looked forward to the spring carnival. The first thing I did at the carnival was buy a funnel cake. I was addicted. Maybe it was the white powdered sugar or the grease but whatever it was, I knew I would start the carnival off with a happy mouth and a large grin. Most of the rides were tame, but there were a few that guaranteed you would get a second look at that freshly eaten funnel cake. My favorite ride was the Rock-O-Plane. The egg shaped cage barely held two people and that's assuming the riders were small and hadn't eaten too many funnel cakes. What I like about the Ferris-wheel type ride was the lap bar with a round "steering wheel" that when you pulled back on it, you would flip backwards and continue to flip until you released the lever. I never released the lever. If you rode the Rock-O-Plane with me, you were going to spin the entire ride. Years later, as an adult on a business trip to St Louis, I had a few hours to kill between meetings.

I wanted to see what the inside of the arch looked like. That idea proved to be a Rock-O-Plane flashback. The basement of the St. Louis Arch is a large museum that I found to be less stimulating than I had hoped for. Walking around, I noticed a line of people. When you see a line there's usually something interesting, so I walked over to see why people were lining up. The sign read, "See St. Louis" from the top of the arch.

Interesting. I got in line. I had no idea there was no elevator.

When the time came that I could see exactly what I was in for, I hesitated but decided what the heck and stayed in line. The employee motioned me and the people in line near me to step forward. "Five at a time, please."

When the small door opened I got flashbacks of the Rock-O-Plane. The same sized cage and it was expected to carry five of us. I scanned my traveling partners and the five of us were basically the same size. As we gathered into the small egg shaped transport, I knew it was going to be very crowded and tight. Kneecap to kneecap, strangers became intimate. The guy next to me had just eaten garlic. When the hatch like door was closed, for the first time in my life I felt claustrophobic. No windows, a very small Christmas light lit the confined area. I held my breath. His garlic smell got stronger. Rather than the egg transport zip us up like an elevator, it moved slowly, making a clicking sound with each forward motion. We were definitely moving upwards, six inches at a click.

It seemed like forever, one click at a time, to make it to the top. There was no "steering wheel" to make the egg shaped cage flip backwards. No funnel cake to distract you. Just you and four other people, all heads down not looking into each other's eyes and seeing the same fear that was ripping at your very being. The hatch door opened and each one of us literally had to unfold our body to get out. A birth canal is bigger.

Once at the top, standing for a moment and letting the feeling come back in my legs, I walked to the center of the arch. It is actually a hallway-like span at the tallest part of the arch. To see the city and not just look at the clouds, you had to lean forward, lay your chest on a carpeted large window sill to look out. You do get the sense of tumbling forward especially when you feel the entire structure sway in the wind. That's right. That sucker eased back and forth, a lot more than I was comfortable with. To be honest, I had the strange feeling that a funnel cake was about to re-appear, even though it had been years since I had eaten one.

It wasn't until a few minutes later that I realized there's only one way up and the same way down. Rock-O-Plane. The sight of the city was awesome but I was ready for my feet to touch ground earth. The swaying in the wind thing was too strange. I lingered near the Rock-O-Plane cage until there were only two occupants and no line waiting. I lunged forward. Three occupants of the tiny cage was a lot better than five. I swore that day that the St. Louis Arch is a onetime event for me. Besides, they didn't have funnel cakes or an outdoor exit with cardboard boxes.

It's not always how you ride, but what you ride.

Traditionally Polite

Southern traditions are plentiful. Some are enjoyable, like the forty-five minutes of hugging when departing from a large family gathering. Everybody hugs, do-si-do, everybody hugs someone else. It's expected, it's anticipated and by gum if you skip someone, you can bet they get their feelings hurt. It's who we are and what we do. And, it's what we see as we grow up and pass along to our kids and their kids. Hugging, no matter what else is going on in the world, will never end. It's sort of like leaving a family reunion. The hugging has no end.

One tradition, I guess I may never understand, is that last biscuit. No one will eat it, no matter what. It doesn't matter that your mouth is set on it. It doesn't matter that you are still hungry. You simply do not eat the last piece of chicken left on the platter. If you eat that last cinnamon roll, your life will be cursed for the rest of your days. The last donut in a now worn Shipley box will be better served hitting the trash rather than folks claiming you to be the family glutton. Seeing folks off; you feel obligated to stand in the driveway until they pull out of sight. It's expected. It's considered polite of you.

Don't take your hand down from waving bye, not until your company is no longer in sight. And if you turn off the porch light before they get to the end of the driveway, it's like saying, "Good Riddance." Nope. The light stays on, the hand continues to wave until tail lights fade in the distance.

Southerners are into feelings. Feelings touch the soul and we go out of our way to avoid hurting them. We eat their crappy banana pudding and pretend it's the best-ever. We drink their weak iced tea and compliment on how refreshing the tea is. No one can set up a fine glass of iced sweet tea like Aunt Mabel.

Thing is, Aunt Mabel lost her sense of taste just before her eighty-seventh birthday. But Bless her heart, we can't tell her that her sweet tea taste like dishwater. That would hurt her feelings and that's something we just won't do.

I went to a friend's house and was told his grandmother had been in the kitchen since early morning perfecting her authentic Italian meatballs and sauce. Either my tongue was going to taste something familiar that says enjoy or appeal to the part that says run. If this is authentic, give me the step down version. I don't want to chew basil.

What we do is set ourselves up, because of traditions. We praise the unworthy and thereby perpetuate, even encourage foods that the dog wouldn't feed her puppies. Most good Southerners know that dogs don't taste, they just eat. But, when they won't eat it, find a large planter that needs fertilizing.

There's high ground. There is salvation, if you don't mind a small white lie. You can all of a sudden develop an allergy to authentic Italian spaghetti sauce, or you can claim your blood sugar has dropped and you need the sugar in that last doughnut. The important thing is to be careful not to hurt someone's feelings because after all, you might be the one making the spaghetti sauce.

When you have company leaving, claim it's too hot or too cold to stand outside on the door step until they are out of sight. I've always wondered what people do in the car once they get in. It's not like they are about to embark on a space mission and have to check all of the dials and buttons on the flight panel. It's a car; turn the key, crank it up, put it in gear and adios.

Loved having you but don't make us swat unnecessary mosquitoes or stand in a light rain to watch you leave. Have the courtesy to exceed the speed limit out of the driveway.

Gain that respected distance so we can go back in the house where we can watch the last three minutes of a movie that we've invested two hours in. Southerner's thrive on their traditions. There are many. Most are cordial, some are just plain silly. But we follow protocol and end up missing the game's kick off.

In reality, our traditions began in hopes of comforting someone, certainly to avoid hurting anyone's feelings. Sometimes it's okay to miss the kick off. Sometimes we drink the dishwater tea, but we always, not some times, avoid hurting someone's feelings. Smile and endure.

Pass that last donut and turn off the porch light.

My Mississippi

Being land-locked in a small Southern town brings to mind the very first time I stood before the Gulf Coast, with my mouth gaping and rendered speechless at the vast, endless aqua blueness of such a large body of water. Larger than anything I've ever seen before, leaving a person feeling mighty small.

Never mind the busy shrimpers and fisherman readying their boats or just returning from a long day's work. Never mind the people that drove by as if there were no Gulf. Never mind the first time seeing crane like birds diving into the water for their dinner. Palm trees, buildings that are taller than any I've ever seen before and endless traffic on the most narrow road that runs parallel to the Gulf of Mexico. This body of water is huge and the activity around it is constant.

The air smelled fresh, with a heavy sent of salt and the skies appeared to be larger, vaster, clearer and bluest of blue. We have a lesser blue sky back home. Obviously, home is Greenville, Mississippi. A small, energetic town destined for greatness. With her lakes, ponds, and of course the Mississippi River, she is no stranger to waterways, although she is land-locked. There are stark differences of her brownish, murky waters to the crystal clear, beautiful greenish-blue waters of the Mississippi Gulf Coast. I wonder if it's the salt in the water that better reflects the sky's blueness. It's the first time I remember seeing water that you can actually see depth, rocks on the bottom, fish swimming and all of the ocean's creatures moving about beneath.

Our mighty Mississippi River conceals her treasures with a murkiness that is hard to see beyond the top water's surface. Maybe that's why we grow record catfish. It's also the reason and origin for grappling.

Why a fella would be willing to stick his hands deep into murky waters and into dead hollowed trees in hopes of pulling out a thirty pound catfish is beyond my reasoning. There are far too many underwater creatures that lay in wait to get a bite of a human.

On the Coast, it makes better sense to grapple. At least, you have some vision where your hands are going. Seems to me there's a better likelihood of getting your hand back.

I remember my first shrimp Po-boy on the Coast. To me, there's no better sandwich than a fresh shrimp Po-boy. Although, I have to say, a half-pound bacon, lettuce, tomato and mayo is a tight second. More often than not, a BLT becomes first choice, given the shortage of fresh shrimp in our land-locked town.

The Gulf is magnificent at land's end of our beautiful state. There are countless strategic places that one can rest the body and still the mind. To me, that's the advantage of the Gulf Coast. Getting lost in her vastness and beauty one can find a quietness and peace that slows the heartbeat and eases whatever is on your mind.

On a recent trip to the Coast a good friend, Danny Thomas, took me to Mikey's, a small eatery in Ocean Springs. Danny knows his shrimp Po-boys. Mikey's serves, hands down, the best you could ever set your mouth for.

Imagine, if you will, an ideal afternoon of cruising with a friend down the narrow highway that runs alongside the Gulf. You are riding shotgun in an antique Corvette that can snatch a knot in your neck in first and second gear. Top down, the salty sea breeze blows the few remaining locks that age hasn't yet erased and basking in a pure sun unrestricted without smog and factory smoke. The sound of the waves splashing against the rocks and the purr of the engine as the corvette speeds around the winding curves in the road. Head back, eyes closed, soaking up the natural sun, breathing in the salty air and loving the moment. Life is good!

Its times like this that need to be savored, stored in the memory banks.

I love my Mississippi River, and Lakes Lee, Washington and Ferguson but I have to tell you there's a another kind of love. The Gulf Coast has a different attack to the senses. The great part of it is, that I have the opportunity to drive from my home, at the tip-top most Northern city in our State, the entire length to the Southern most cities...and never, not once, not for a moment, leave Mississippi. Everything from the top with the rich fertile lands of the Delta to rivers and streams and large bodies of water to the Gulf of Mexico with its seafood at the bottom, it's all Mississippi, unique, engaging, and memorable.

For example, in a tiny, one red light hamlet just south of Florence there is a curbside market that has everything you can imagine, canned. We're talking the Great Generation type canning of anything that can be grown or raised. It's a real throw back of surviving off the land. If there's ever a shortage of food, I know where I am headed, "Maters and Taters."

The owner had spent the morning shucking corn and cutting it off the cob. Who does that? His wife had spent her morning preparing plums for the most delicious plum jelly that will grace a hot-from-the-oven, homemade biscuit. These people will survive while the rest of us forage for the last few items left on Kroger's shelf.

They are land-locked. They aren't mind-locked. Therein lays the pioneer spirit of our State. The vast beautiful Gulf is nature's food store where you can find fish, shrimp, oysters and crabs.

The Gulf's bounty has fed humans since time began. Equally, the land-locked have found their provisions from the richest soil on earth, the Mississippi Delta sandy loam. We may do without some things, but food and the pioneer spirit doesn't make that list. We are survivors. We fight our way through Coastal storms and land-locked tornadoes. Our resilience bounces us back stronger, learning nature's lessons to help us get through the next one.

Our State, the State of Mississippi has anything and everything we want need or desire, except honest politicians. We are one of the most corrupt states and for good cause. Our State's natural resources and inventive minds are too much of a temptation for corrupt politics.

No place is perfect, but our state is as close as you can get. If it were not for the slick willies always out to beat the system, depriving our State of her birthright, we for sure, would be at the top of the list.

We can out-wrong the worst of the New York's and LA's of the country, starting at dog catcher to Mayor to the State's highest political offices.

That's our hold back. When we get rid of the riffraff and crooked snakes from the flat sandy loam of the Delta to the Gulf and all in between, Mississippi, like her namesake, will become Mighty.

Mississippi politics needs a purple enema.

Coming Home

The first home I remember is 202 Alexander. The intersection of Alexander and Walnut Street ends at the foot of the levee.

It was "Big," a grand old house. Mom and Dad rented out four apartments and we occupied the fifth apartment. While I didn't know it, I was getting an education in a being landlord. But that comes later. Next door to us at 206 Alexander was Jerry Brown and his family. Across the street were the Swilley's and Tobia's.

Duke Tobia, and I would spend most every daylight hour on the levee romping, running, sliding on cardboard boxes, and acting out the most recent cowboy movie we had seen at the Lake Theater or Paramount. One of my favorite things to do was to lie on my back and watch the clouds slowly change forms as they bumped into each other or disappeared. It's amazing what shapes you can make out from each cloud drifting by. I would try to show Duke what cloud looks like a bear and he would try to point out "his" cloud that looks like a rabbit. It was as much fun finding shapes as it was trying to see what shape Duke found. Sometimes we would just lay still, not talk or hunt each other's shapes in the clouds. Good friends can do that. They don't always have to be running, or in a great debate as to which one is going to be the Indian and the other the cowboy.

Duke was a good friend, talking or not. We are three weeks a part in age. Friendships that are made at that age never fade. Today, fifty years later Duke and I can meet up and talk like we spent yesterday together.

I don't see him as often as I'd like but when we do get together, I am that six year old kid that lived next to the levee and had a buddy that walked the top of the levee looking for

Coke and Pepsi bottles that people threw out of their cars. We used the deposit money paid to us by Mr. Williams at William's Grocery at the corner of Alexander and Poplar Streets, to go to the movies.

Movies were a big deal for us. We'd watch Roy Rogers or Hop-Along Cassidy Movies and spend the next two weeks re-enacting the story line, alternating the good guy-bad guy roles.

Sometimes, if we had just been to the movies we would use our deposit money to buy a short, ice cold Coke Cola and a handful of large Jack's cookies. You can't buy Cokes that taste that good anymore. My favorite drink then and still is, was a Barq's root beer. I'd take a few swallows first to make room for a pack of peanuts that I'd be slowly funneling in.

Duke and his family moved away from Greenville. I was lost without Duke for a long while. New friendships formed but there never was a replacement for Duke.

Years later, a few weeks after Carol and I married, I went back to the old neighborhood, buying the Brown's home and renting out both apartments. We lived in our honeymoon home that was twenty-five by twenty-five feet, behind the 206 address. It had one bedroom, a bath, living room/dining room and kitchen. Cozy. We spent the next year renovating our little honeymoon cottage.

The front two apartments were a challenge at best, especially for someone who hadn't turned twenty, was in college and worked one full and one part time job. While I learned a great deal watching Mom and Dad manage their apartments, apparently they were much better at choosing tenets that actually paid rent. I, on the other hand, fell for every sob story in the book.

Three years later, we bought our first home away from the old neighborhood on Wasson Drive, across the street from the Tabb's. Jerry Brown and his family settled two houses down from us on Wasson Drive. It's funny how things repeat themselves.

Throughout one's life, people come and go. It is good friendships that anchor into one's being that can come alive after years of being apart. Friends become a part of who you are and that never changes, no matter the distance or time.

If you have a friendship that dates back fifty years, you are truly fortunate.

A good friendship never ends.

Unsinkable

Suffragette would hardly be a term used to describe my grandmother. She neither suffered nor asked for the vote. Fact is, she didn't ask for anything, she demanded it.

Born in Kansas City in 1897, the tenth of fourteen children to immigrant parents who entered the U.S. in 1880, she became a self-made, determined, wealthy woman that commanded a cottage industry that she built, and managed on her own, never stopping to wait for permission.

When she was six years old, her dad, never completely happy with leaving his homeland behind, decided he wanted to return. Her mom, a pillar of strength and most probably the template and role model, refused to abandon her dream. She wanted better for herself and her children. The only amiable solution was for him to take seven of their children back to Lebanon, leaving her with seven children and on her own. The divorce was handled by long distance mail. He was never heard from again. Whatever ties there were to her and the old country had been severed.

She took on sewing, washing and whatever she needed to do to care for her seven children. Her husband returned to his homeland with the other seven children, along with my grandmother.

At age eleven, unhappy and miserable, she persisted with the notion of returning to America until her father caved and supplied her with boat passage. Alone, she made the long journey to reconnect with her mother and siblings. Today, we can't imagine an eleven year old crossing the street alone.

What she found wasn't what she had imagined. Life was tough, money scarce and there were a lot of mouths to feed.

Their struggle for survival continued until at age fifteen, she married an older man and found life could get worse. She endured and secretly hid money she made sewing, planning a way out of her unhappy life.

At age twenty, she abandoned the life she was miserable with and moved to a small community just South of Greenville, Mississippi. It's there she realized a dry goods store was needed. With her meager savings she invested everything she had and opened a small store, to an amazing success. She lived in the back of her store.

Alone, young and beautiful and an owner of a business, she drew lots of young men. None suited her and according to her, they only wanted a soft living based on her hard work.

A customer, passing through Arcola, stopped at her store and told her about the housing opportunities in Greenville. On pursuit of an even better life, she visited Greenville, noted there was a housing shortage and begun buying older homes built for large families. With a wall here, a bathroom added there, she split the large, homes into three, sometimes four apartments and rented them out.

Her business model was a rather simple one. "Never use your own money." She would take out a small loan with the lowest interest rate, usually extended to only the very rich. She was a tough negotiator and never compromised. She was relentless and backed up quite a few bank presidents to agree to her terms.

In less than five years she owned ten houses that were split into about forty apartments. The rent collected paid off her loans in short order. The dry goods store in Arcola was flourishing. She sold it for an amazing profit and moved closer to her new business in Greenville, buying more homes and restructuring them into apartments. Greenville was on the boom, moving forward and low income families needed a place to live. She supplied the demand. Her "empire" grew at a fast pace. She never, not once considered failure as her property numbers grew.

Before the age of thirty she was a wealthy landlord and had more gentlemen callers than she wanted to deal with. They were consistent in what she called a soft living based on her hard work. She married a few of them only to find her fears were correct. They wanted a free ride and free rides didn't exist in her world. She didn't linger in those doomed relationships.

In one such doomed marriage, although her husband was a dynamic businessman, they butted heads often. Eventually, neither of them were happy and they parted their ways. She had three sons in that marriage, Dad was the middle child.

Much like her doomed marriages and her fear of some guy living off of her, she was careful not to coddle her boys. They earned their way from an early age. She was never what one would call generous. She had hardened over the years because of bad marriages and a string of freeloaders. She demanded her boys have backbone and would not tolerate laziness.

Of the many homes she owned one stood out more than the others. It was 831 South Broadway. A three story Victorian home obviously built at the turn of the century by an extremely wealthy man. When she gained ownership, the home was older, needed repair and was promptly turned into six apartments. The roof line was metal and she thought a silver roof was in order. The rest of the home was painted a loud, talk back to you, pink. She called it her pink palace. The carefully made apartments were striking. Hand carved mantel pieces adorned the imported marble fireplaces. Faces and scenes were all hand carved to exquisite details. The hand carved staircase was a living piece of art. 831 South Broadway was her dream home. She had arrived and finally bought the home she could almost relax in. Aged at this point, she never slowed down, doing roofing, structure rebuilding, slicing one family houses into apartments, mostly on her own, and doing the heavy lifting.

She had hired carpenters, plumbers and handymen, but she oversaw every project, making sure workers were earning their salaries. Often she would fire them and swing a hammer herself, if they moved to slow.

At age eighty I recall seeing her on a roof, laying tar paper and setting up the roof to be tiled. She never stopped working, replacing a water heater in her mid-eighties and could still swing a hammer better than most professional carpenters.

831 S. Broadway calmed her, or maybe it was her age, or a combination of both. Whatever caused it, I don't know, but she slowed a bit; unless there was a bank president that needed a good talking to, or a plumber that didn't fix the problem. Her younger self emerged when she felt the need. The flames may have been burning lower but the heat from the fire remained white-hot, until the day she left this earth.

She was a role model for any woman that wanted better and was willing to take on the man's world. She never blinked. She never backed away. She stood her ground on major as well as minor issues. She never tried to be a man but she never found a man her equal.

She didn't believe in hanging on to the past. The past was done and she never looked back. She seldom spoke Lebanese or referenced her family in the old country. They were the past. She broke the ties to the old country and focused her attention to the future.

My dad called her a tough old bird. He was right. She came up tough, lived a tough life and remained tough until her last days, never giving in on the most minute of details. She was headstrong, determined and unflinching.

I've seen her sit at a wooden table she built herself and hammer out used nails back to almost straight, to be re-used on one of her remodels. She had a large room in her home that would shame any hardware store, mostly filled with used plumbing, electrical items and used wood. She never allowed any waste.

In her last years I can remember her sitting at a foot pumped, Singer sewing machine, the very one she used to make a living in her teen years, still sewing her own dresses. She was in her late eighties and refused to buy store bought dresses, even though she could have easily bought every dress store in Greenville...and then some.

She was a remarkable woman. Hardened, yes, but if you took an honest, deep, unflinching look at the parents of the Greatest Generation, one gets a better understanding of what made the Greatest Generation, great.

She was there. She was front line in Greenville's formation, along with Jake Stein and other notables that grew Greenville. She was usually, the only woman in the room. She was the unsinkable "Miss Mary."

Her favorite expression, "Make excuses or make money."

The Greatest Generation didn't just happen.

BUTLAWA

Here is the recipe everyone has been asking for.

Baklava as the Greeks call it, Butlawa is how we know it.

I've placed it at the back of the book so you can find it easily, when you are ready to try out this incredible dessert.

Well before you are ready to begin, take the phillo dough from your freezer and allow it to thaw.

Here's what you need;

1 pkg. of fillo dough. Also spelled phillo or phyllo. Normally found in the freezer section, next to frozen pies.

1 c. coarsely ground pecans

¼ tsp rose water. This ingredient isn't that common unless you shop an International store or a Mediterranean store. It is absolutely required. If you can't find it locally, you can order it on the internet. One bottle will last you years.

1/3 pound of sweet/unsalted butter, melted. We always use Land of Lakes

2 tsp. of regular sugar

Sugar syrup (topping, glaze)

1 c. regular sugar

¾ c. water

½ tsp. lemon juice

1 tsp. rose water

Mix ground pecans, 2 tsp sugar, and ¼ tsp rose water in a separate bowl.

Carefully unwrap the thawed phillo dough and lay flat. Cover with a towel to prevent air from hitting the thin dough. If it dries out, it becomes crumbly and difficult to work with.

Lift one sheet of phillo dough, recover the remaining stack. Lay the one sheet on a flat surface, cutting board or counter top and quickly "paint" the melted butter on the sheet, covering all corners.

Remove the next sheet from the stack and lay directly on top of the first sheet and "paint the second layer with the melted butter. Continue this process until you have four sheets each buttered and atop each other.

Add 2 tbsp. of the pecan/sugar mixture, starting an inch or so from the bottom edge spreading across left to right a small continuous mound, leaving an inch or so on each side. Then carefully pull up the bottom edge and roll forward away from you until the wrap is completed. You will have a long "hot dog" shape that you will place in a flat cookie sheet and "paint" another layer of butter on the final roll. Then with a sharp knife, slice into two, three inch servings at a 45 degree angle. Continue until you have seven or eight long hot dogs shaped forms and the stuffing is all used.

Place in an oven at 350 for about 20 minutes, depending on your oven. When there is a rich browning of your butlawa, it is done. Watch this stage very closely Butter burns quickly and easily, as does the phillo dough. Generally twenty minutes is the right bake time.

Preparing the simple sugar glaze.

While your butlawa is baking, in a small sauce pan, add 1 cup water and ¾ cup of regular sugar. Stir to move sugar off bottom. Once you have a boil, add ½ teaspoon of lemon juice. Reduce heat to low and allow it to simmer for fifteen minutes. Remove from heat and add 1 tsp. of rose water. Allow to set.

When the baking is complete, remove from the oven and immediately pour the sugar glaze over the hot butlawa, making sure each piece gets a thin coating. Allow to cool for an hour, before serving.

It sounds complicated. It isn't. Do it in stages. Follow the recipe and enjoy one of the world's best desserts.

THANK YOU!

It's been my pleasure writing memories from a golden time and a priceless childhood. If I've made you smile, and caused you to revisit some of your childhood memories, then I have completed my mission.

Visit me on my Facebook page, Cornbread Memories, and share some of your childhood memories. I also invite your emails at ronkattawar@aol.com

If you've enjoyed the book, "Cornbread Memories 2", please share the ordering site via Amazon with friends and family or send them to my Facebook page. Everyone is welcome! Both books can be ordered from any book store or book store chain or can be ordered via Amazon.

If you missed book one, "Cornbread Memories," paperback and eBooks remain available.

Thank you and enjoy the Cornbread!

Ron Kattawar

Made in the USA
Las Vegas, NV
07 September 2021